A Pilgrimage Without End

A Pilgrimage Without End

How Cancer Healed My Broken Heart

Cherie Rineker

ISBN : 1533464316
ISBN-13: 9781533464316

Cover Illustrations by Greg Whitcoe
Editing by Neshama Abrahams
1st Edition 2016

I dedicate this book to

My son
I loved you from the moment I held you
and wished I had never let you go.

My daughter
Sweetheart, without you I surely would
have lost the will to go on.

My mother
For better or worse, you have shaped my life
in more ways than you can ever imagine,
and for that I am eternally grateful.

My husband
For being there through sickness and
health, for better or worse.
Honey, I could not have done this without you!

Let me, this day be in attunement
with all Love and all Light.
Let me be a channel of that Love, that
Light to those I meet in every way.
Let my thoughts and desires be in
alignment with Loving Energy.
Each and every day

Table of Content

Foreword

I hope you will find Cherie to be as engaging an author as I have. Her tale is intimately personal. Cherie shares the deepest part of herself, her struggles and the lessons she has learned along the way. Her story is not just another autobiographical journal of her battle with cancer." *A Pilgrimage Without End*" is much more than that! It is a well-crafted, self-examination from which we all can learn. In it she reveals her deepest, and often darkest, emotional, physical, and spiritual struggles she has faced throughout her life. Much of what she has to say is relevant to all of us, and not just those facing a battle with cancer. More than this, Cherie's self-examination and search for truth provides the reader with practical and spiritual guidance and insight when facing their own struggles. Thus, her story is one from which we all can benefit, whether we are confronting cancer, emotional struggles, or life changing events. Read it and be blessed.

- Nicholas Calderon, JD.

Preface

Because this book contains sensitive material, I decided to change the names and places in order to protect the identities of those that were part of shaping my life. This book is not a book that wishes to put anybody in a bad light. Yet in order to be able to help others I did feel it important to share some of the difficult times I experienced. I hope that by doing so I can help those that are dealing with similar issues and give them hope and inspiration.

I want to be clear that I in no way claim to have all the answers to happiness and inner peace. Ever since I was a child I was a seeker. I came into this world a philosopher, always pondering life's bigger questions, always looking for answers. I have tried many different ways of living. My desire to learn and understand other people and cultures has shaped my life in such a way that I acquired a high level of tolerance and acceptance of other people's views.

When I was a little girl my father told me a story about his experience as an officer in the British Merchant Marines. He told us that, during his layovers in China, the Chinese workers would empty their nose by covering one nostril and blowing the mucus straight out on the street. When my father questioned one of them about this rather strange and disgusting behavior, the Chinese worker told him that he thought it rather gross for people to have a handkerchief in their pocket in which they would blow their noses, wrap the booger up as if it were some kind of treasure and carefully put it back into their pocket. This way of looking at different points of views set the tone for me to understand that there is not just one way of looking at the world.

Traditional Japanese etiquette expects their guests to finish their plate, in appreciation of the food offered. At the same time, in some cultures, cleaning your plate is interpreted as if you did not get enough to eat. In these cultures, it is preferred that you leave a little food on your plate to show you were given plenty.

When I was a flight attendant we were taught to serve our passengers from the back of the airplane to the front, from the window to the aisle. However, if the couple was American we had to serve "ladies first", regardless of where she sat. If, on the other hand, the couple was

Japanese, we had to serve the man first, regardless of where he sat, and if the person was from the Middle East we had to serve him with our right hand only, as the left hand was considered unclean and used for "personal" business.

I really appreciated knowing these etiquette traditions, as I did not want to offend anybody. On the other hand, I believed it important for people to understand our culture as well, and to be forgiving if we did not know their rules. It seemed wrong to me for a Japanese couple, or a person from the Middle East to feel insulted if I, a Westerner, forgot to use the appropriate etiquette because they too should be aware of our rules and customs.

The reason I am sharing this with you is to explain why, for me, there is not much that is either "right" or "wrong" in this world. There is perception and interpretation, but to make things "wrong" is to judge and that is never good. It is not "wrong" to leave food on our plates, nor to finish every last crumb. Tradition is wonderful, and if you wish to live according to your own traditions then go right ahead. Just don't insist others to live according to your rules as well.

Free Will, has been our biggest gift. For me, as long as my Free Will does not hurt or infringe on your Free

Will, we are good and there should be no reason why we can't all get along and live together in Peace. And remember, let us be kind to each other…. Always!!!

With Love and Light,

Cherie Rineker
Houston, Texas, May 22, 2016

Acknowledgements

During my journey with cancer, Facebook brought so many wonderful people into my life. When I was stuck on the couch, or during the many stays and treatments in the hospital, too sick to go anywhere or even talk on the phone, Facebook allowed me to stay in touch with those I loved. Social media has been a stepping stone into the public world for me. It has allowed me to reach out when I was in pain and needed comfort. It brought back many forgotten friendships from my childhood, and healed wounds that never could have healed otherwise.

Greg Whitcoe, thank you for putting together my website, book cover, and amazing pictures. You are a genius and I hope the world will get to know your work better.

Nancy Hallinger, thank you for doing the initial edit. Your help gave me the confidence to know that I was on the right track.

Neshama Abrahams, thank you the final edit of my book. You brought me to Boulder, CO where I was able to safely finish the last month of my cannabis trial. Your hospitality was more than I could have asked for, and I will forever treasure our friendship.

I want to thank all my neighbors who so caringly checked in on me, drove me to my many doctors' appointments, or just came to sit with me and cheer me up. Thank you everybody, for always helping me with Naomi, taking her to piano and gymnastics, or simply keeping her for hours so I could rest. They say it takes a village to raise a child. I know this has certainly been the case in my life.

Introduction

*M*y desire to write this book has been with me for many years. I have met people from all over the world, and because it is in my nature to trust I felt safe to share my story. Many who heard it suggested I turn my experiences into a book. My desk is full of thoughts written in binders, diaries, even on napkins. Several years ago I started writing my first book. When I was about 50 pages into the book my computer crashed, destroying everything I had written. Instead of getting upset, I realized I was not ready to tell my story yet. You see, in those days I just wanted to write down the pain that surrounded my childhood. It was really just a whine fest, wrapped in some spiritual phrases and words that I had learned along the way. In those days I had read about different ways to get to peace and happiness, but I was lousy at implementing them.

This book will open your eyes to the issue of emotional child abuse. It may be uncomfortable for some, as you may feel you are the perpetrator of that abuse. It is not my intent to make anybody feel guilty. It is not my intent to demonize my parents. It is, however, my desire to let people know that what they believe is okay to do or say to their children can cause wounds that may take a lifetime to heal.

Many of us feel lost in life, for all kinds of reasons. We often feel like victims, like the world, our parents, our children, spouses, boyfriends, you name it, have let us down. We reach for self-help books to "fix" our problems, to "fix" the other person and ourselves. Whenever I'd read a book that promised me answers I would become excited about fixing the situation around and inside of me. Yet soon I would be let down by my inability to put into practice what I had just read. On top of this the other people in my life did not cooperate with my new-found knowledge. If only they would react as the book told me they would! Yet this never seemed to be the case.

I tried religion, many kinds and many times. I have been "saved" several times, with the promise of never feeling alone again, yet this wasn't true for me either. The more I tried and failed, the worse I felt. Though I had many "aha" moments I simply could not fill that deep hole in my heart that was left from my childhood. It took a cancer diagnosis for me to find myself, and to truly let go of the pain that had gripped me for nearly four decades.

I am writing this book to offer hope to those who struggle with similar issues, to show others that it is indeed possible to heal deep childhood wounds. This place of inner peace exists in everyone, and it does not require a perfect life or body to achieve. These days I spend a lot of my time on the couch nursing my aching body, yet I feel happier and more at peace than I ever have. There are many paths that lead us to happiness but, in the end, we are the only ones in the driver's seat and we are the responsible party of our life's story.

This time I did not write a book to get sympathy. I wrote this book because somehow, somewhere along the way I learned how to love and accept myself. Like a diet it was a slow process. For me there was no "Secret" movie, pill or book, though the many books I read over the years certainly helped me. What worked for me was an unwillingness to merely survive. I had a deep burning desire to make my life better and heal my soul. I knew the pain of my past was eating me up, something that was confirmed when I was diagnosed with Multiple Myeloma in November 2012.

My approach to life is to be open and willing to learn. This was the only way I managed to survive when I ran away at age 17. Since I had been judged so harshly by my mother, I was determined not to do the same to others. I checked out many different ways of life, searching for the one that would fit me best. I hope my readers will not be offended by my journey and subsequent conclusions. Please stay with my story so you can understand how it brought me to the place I am today. I embrace people's choices about pretty much anything in life. Judgment, because I felt its nasty affects, is something I have tried my hardest to stay clear of. This does not mean that I don't observe. As a matter of fact, I watch people very closely. I try to understand where people are coming from and why they believe the way they do. I believe we are pure of heart when we come into this world. It is life's circumstances that ends up shaping our thoughts and actions.

It is my desire to try and understand why people think and act the way they do, and how we can all get along despite our differences. Many people do not give their lives, or their actions a lot of thought. They just go with the cards life has dealt them, and try to survive. Surviving is what I had to do for many years, and it simply wasn't good enough anymore. I wanted to live and thrive!

My biggest advice to you: **show up authentic every day!** Forget about fitting in and being liked by everybody, because that is simply not going to happen. Remember to be gentle with yourself. The wounds you are healing did not show up overnight, nor will they likely disappear in a day. Be bold and try different ways to heal. Step out of your comfort zone, push the envelope! Remember, the values taught to you by your parents came from people as imperfect as you are. You aren't disrespecting your elders by wanting to try a different route. This is *your* life; **you** get to decide how to live it.

One thing that is an absolute must is HOPE!!! You must allow yourself to believe in anything and everything! Just because your life up to now feels like a failure, does not mean tomorrow can't be better. Remember, this is not a blame game. Don't be hard on yourself or those you feel have wronged you. Yet as a dear friend of mine said, "If you get run over by a truck.... your injuries are indeed caused by that truck and that cannot and should not be denied!" Know, therefore, that you cannot heal a wound which you do not acknowledge.

Cherie Rineker

"I have never been given anything I could not handle."

1

Why Me?

The doctor on duty in the Emergency Room at Saint Luke's Hospital in Tempe, Arizona walked in and without looking at me said, "Well, you are severely anemic and you have cancer." I was physically comfortable for the first time in 6 months. The attending nurse had given me morphine an hour earlier. What an incredible rush that was! I have never done heroin but I have seen enough scenes in the movies leading me to believe that my initial rush must have been similar. My friend Greg and I had been joking around, so I looked at the doctor smiling and said, "You are joking, right?" His face was very serious as he looked at me and said he did not joke about things like this. In that moment, I felt my life fall apart. As I broke down in tears I felt a fear I had never felt before. I wanted to scream and run from the perpetrator, yet knowing it was inside of me there was nowhere to run. This moment will stay with me for as long as I live. It is one of those moments we have felt collectively, like when President Kennedy was assassinated or when our country was attacked on 9/11. How could this have happened...... to me!!!

My life had been far from easy up to that point. I guess that is what happens when one comes from a difficult childhood, where the abuse, both physical and emotional, is very difficult to handle, especially for a sensitive child like me. My mother was a very unhappy and judgmental woman. She felt she did not fit in with the British, the country my father had brought her to. My mother was born and raised in Panama on a tea plantation. My father and mother met while he was an officer in the British merchant marines and she was going to nursing school. They went out for only three days, after which he had to leave and continue on his route. They promised to write each other. My father proposed to my Mom in one of his letters and they got married one year after they first met. My father always told me, "One can do only two things well in life. If you pick more than two things, you can't be good at any of them." Dad picked his work and his wife, and there was little or no room left for us kids. Why they chose to have five children in a country that on average has less than two per family is something I never quite understood, especially since Mom seemed so obviously unhappy with her job of being a mother.

I did not know my father well. He often got up after we left for school, and he preferred us kids in bed when he came home in the evening. My parents had a very old fashioned marriage where my father was expected to bring home the money and pay the bills, and my mother pretty much did the rest. My father would proudly say that he did not know how to boil water, while my mother probably never saw a check in her life. My parents wanted a son and had his name already picked out before they were married. It just so happened that four girls were born before he finally showed up. We girls had to do a lot around the house, something that came from my mother's Central American upbringing. My brother's childhood was completely different from ours. We considered him to be very spoiled. He did not have to do work around the house like we had to, nor was he punished in the way we were. He was also given much more freedom. Looking back, his was a more normal childhood, one I ended up giving to my own children.

My mother often told me how her life would have been better if she had not had us girls. It hurts when your mother calls you a "parasite," or a "biological mistake." My father always told us not to take the words my mother said too seriously, that she was merely a passionate woman and that she did not mean the hurtful things she said to us. Still, as a child, and even when I was a grown woman, that sense of being a burden and never being good enough stayed with me. When my oldest, sister ran away from home at age 14, followed by my other sister being kicked out at age 18, while still in high school, I thought it was my only option to run away myself at the tender age of 17, when I felt I, too, had become a disappointment to my mother.

I was a bright student and a good kid. I did not smoke, drink or do drugs. Yet I had become a "wild" child in my mother's eyes, simply because I no longer agreed with everything she said. I never *meant* to run away, I had always been on my mother's side, feeling her pain, but as I got older, I started to see more and more how unreasonable she was, and how her punishments never fit the crime.

Summer vacation had just started. I was 17 ½ and in love with Peter, my first "real" boyfriend. We were allowed to go out, and as teenagers often do, we forgot about the time. Knowing how mad my parents would be, I called them prior to my curfew and told them we would be home 15 minutes late. My father told me to just come home and hung up. I knew I was in serious trouble!

We always had to come home right after school, not being allowed to hang out with the other kids. This rigidness became harder as we got older and in those few instances that we chose to hang around with our classmates we would be grounded for a month. Although the bicycle ride home usually took about 25 minutes, my boyfriend and I did it in 15. I felt something would be terribly wrong, so I asked him to stay by the road until I found out what my punishment was going to be. I knocked on the door and my mother let me in and told me to go to bed. After she went back into her room I ran to the street and told Peter that everything was okay. But when I tried to get back into the house, my mother had locked me out. I banged on the door several times and when I realized that my punishment would be a night out in the cold I ran after Peter barefoot and told him I was tired of it all and wanted to come home with him. I had seen so much drama with my two older sisters and, at 17 years old, I did not feel like putting up with the same stuff. I rode on the back of his bike but when we got to his house his parents told me I could not stay. They called my parents who told me to get a cab and come home. They would punish me in the morning. The next day I was told that I was not to leave the house for the rest of the summer and that I could not see Peter. He was not even allowed to call me! It would be my job to stay home and clean the house. I was furious! It was the beginning of my summer break and I was grounded for the entire two months. Here I was 17 and I could not go anywhere!! For the first time in my life I was really angry at my parents.

We all have our ways of raising our children. Some of us are tougher than others and that is okay. To each their own. I will just say that for those parents who might be quite strict, beware you don't do to your children what my parents did to me. I believe in parenting with clear limits concerning things like safety, respect and education, but mostly I parent through positive reinforcement, leniency and Love. A more forgiving and loving approach has been proven to work better, for animals, children, even spouses. Nobody wants to be nagged or punished. But if we are kind to each other our children will learn the same kind of behavior through our actions and therefore become more compassionate adults. The way I see it, the only way to world peace is to raise our children with lots of Love not only for themselves, but for others as well. We must teach them through example. A child does not listen to the words of his/her parents as much as he/she watches their actions. It was because of my mother's words and actions that I went into the big world with a lot stacked against me. It was because of her inappropriate punishments that she drove her children away.

For the next several days my parents watched me like a hawk. I remember wanting to go to bed at night, and my father throwing me back into my chair, not wanting to take his eyes off me for fear of me running away as my older sister had done so many times before. I remember waking up in the morning to find my mother sitting on the couch making sure I would not leave. One day I defiantly put one foot outside the fence and my mother grabbed me by the hair and dragged me into my bedroom where she threw me on the bed and got ready to hit me. I told her to go ahead, so that I would have evidence to show to child protective services. I no longer cared. I hated my mother at that point. I had never felt or spoken like that. I surprised myself with the pent up anger I felt. The next morning, when my father went off to work I ran downstairs in my jeans, shoes and a white sweater, grabbed my bike and took off with my mother yelling after me. That night I wanted to come home, but I was scared. I never disobeyed my parents like this before, *ever*! If I was grounded for the summer for being 15 minutes late, what would they do to me now? Ground me until I was 30!

During this time, I worked as a waitress at a pancake restaurant in the next town over. It was a nice authentic pancake house in an old windmill. When walking in you could see two cooks making the best pancakes I have ever tasted. These weren't your everyday pancakes. No, these pancakes were huge! They barely fit on the extra-large plates they came on, deliciously falling over the edge. One could order them with all kinds of fillings that were directly cooked into the pancakes. In the mood for something sweet, you could try apple, banana, and raisins topped off with grand Marnier. If you rather wanted something heartier, then a cheese, onion, bacon, and ham pancake might just be what you were looking for. When the oil, onions and bacon went into the hot stainless steel pan it caused a huge flame several feet up that made for quite a show.

One of the cooks had a crush on me. He lived by himself and told me I could stay with him. Too scared to go home and face the music, I decided to stay with him. Unfortunately, there were strings attached to the stay, something that became my new normal for the next six months until I met my first husband. Even though my parents knew where I worked, they never came looking for me like they had done time and time again for my older sister. I guess they were tired of it all, but to me it felt like I did not matter. To make matters worse there had always been a lot of sibling rivalry in our home between us girls, something my mother fueled rather than controlled. When I told my oldest sister I wanted to come home she said: "Forget it! Mom has told me she does not want you anymore. She said that you might have a chance if you come crawling back to her on your belly begging for forgiveness, but she said she still might send you away!" I was devastated. It was clear to me that my parents no longer wanted me.

I told my mother this story when I was diagnosed with cancer because I wanted to clear all the air between us. I needed to share these things with her as they had shaped my life in such a difficult way. She told me she knew my sister had said that to me but that she had never said those things. I was hurt by the fact that she apparently knew yet did not seem to care. Both actions hurt deeply, that my mother admitted knowing such a heinous lie which had kept me from coming back home when I so desperately wanted and needed to; and the fact that my mother knew about this cruel statement all those years and never reprimanded my sister for something that so damaged my young life. Either way, it was a deep betrayal by my family.

They say blood is thicker than water. Unfortunately, I have lived a life that has been quite the opposite. I have received more Love, help and understanding from strangers than I have ever felt from my family. Without the possibility to come home (or so I thought) I spent those first six months on the streets in Europe, near a town where the American GI's went out at night. Most nights I was able to have a place to sleep and food to eat.

I never sold my body, thankfully most guys are decent and I was often able to talk my way out of it, though not always. On the nights I did not have a place to stay I would wander around or just try to get some sleep in a phone booth. I found a couple of places to stay for longer times, but usually there too, things were "expected" of me.

Why am I telling you all this? After the shock of my diagnosis wore off, I started to try and answer the question, "Why me?" Why did I get Multiple Myeloma, a blood cancer that eats away at the bones? If I try to think about it metaphysically I would say that the bones represent both physical and emotional support. I had never experienced emotional support. Could this have affected my skeletal system? Why would I have gotten this type of cancer, a cancer that typically happens to older people, mainly black men, when the ones least likely to get this condition according to research, are younger women, tall, slender, and vegetarian, all of which I was? Of course this was me trying to find meaning in what happened, something that could never be proven, which is why early on I decided, "Why *not* me?"

"It is amazing what we can handle when we do not have the option to fail!"

2

The Next Step

*B*ack in the emergency room nurses were coming in to calm me down, a couple were crying themselves. It is not every day that a person walks into the Emergency Room with pain symptoms and leaves with a cancer diagnosis. I think we were all in shock. The doctor did not want me to go home. He told me I had three tumors on my spine and one was growing inside my bone marrow. He was surprised I wasn't paralyzed yet. I told him I couldn't go to the hospital, "I have to pick up my 7-year-old daughter, take her home and make her dinner", I explained. I was in complete shock!

Before arriving at the Emergency Room, I had been in unrelenting pain and started to think that cancer was the only disease left that had not yet been ruled out. In between going to school and taking care of my daughter there had been many tests and doctors' visits. Every time a test came back negative I let out a big sigh of relief, yet my symptoms only continued to get worse. Diseases like lupus, valley fever, even AIDS had been ruled out and that scary little "C" word had started to creep in. "Of course you don't have cancer," a friend told me just one month earlier at my daughter's 7th birthday party. "Look at you," she said, "You look healthy, you live and eat healthy, there is no way YOU have cancer! If you do, we are all in trouble!" It was true. I had been living a "healthy" lifestyle for over a decade.

Life had been tough since I ran away from home. After six months I met a nice American GI who was stationed in Europe. We fell in love, and even though the love I felt for him was more one of gratitude than the love that is necessary to sustain a good relationship, we married and had a beautiful baby boy. It turned out we were completely incompatible. My husband was not much of a talker and preferred if I didn't talk either. I was too shy to make friends, and felt stuck in the house with a little baby and not much else. I was barely 18 when I met Robert and he was 8 years older. I think one of the main problems was that I wanted to grow up and therefore change, while he wanted me to stay that insecure quiet girl he met who allowed him to treat her any way he wanted. After seven years I called it quits. By that time, we were based in Grand Forks, North Dakota. Although he promised to stick around and be there for his son who was only one-year-old at the time, Robert took off as soon as he was offered orders to go back to Europe. Orders he certainly could have refused since Grand Forks was always in need of more military personnel. After all, not many air force guys had North Dakota on their dream sheet. He left us in 1993 with a whopping $266 in monthly child support and I was left without family, friends or education.

Life was tough! Sure, I was free of my ex, and his controlling nature and jealousy, but life alone with my son and living in poverty was extremely hard. At that time, I was not the greatest of parents. Because I was afraid of being too strict, I had gone too far the other way, leaving my son without boundaries. He was a handful, yet looking back I can see it was due to my lack of parenting skills. At 23, I was still very much a child myself. The thing is, when a child leaves home too early she is emotionally stuck at the age where she left unless she makes a conscious effort to grow up. I was far from being conscious in those days. I wanted my freedom, I wanted to go out and party and fill that deep void I felt from not having my parents' approval or support.

I remember my son being sick when he was only a few weeks old. He had severe diarrhea and was throwing up for about 48 hours. Even though my mother had refused to see me off when I left Europe, I called home to ask for help. My mother told me that I had made my bed and now had to lie in it, then she hung up on me. I was devastated and felt utterly alone. My husband had tried to do the right thing and asked my parents for my hand in marriage, yet my father had refused; I guess I was being punished for marrying him anyway.

Though I loved my son dearly he stood in the way of the life I thought I wanted to live. With a government grant I went to college. I longed to live like the rest of my classmates, going to class, studying and partying. How I would love to do that time in my life over again, to give my son what he really needed, a Mom who was there for him physically as well as emotionally. Unfortunately, I was so emotionally messed up, there was little to give. Today my son and I have a good relationship. I have apologized to him many times. I gave him the best I could, and I am very aware how much more he deserved and needed. To my daughter's benefit, the trauma of my childhood and the mistakes I made with my son have since made me a very aware and caring mother. I have raised Naomi as I wish I could have been raised myself. She and I have never had a bad moment together. She saved me in more ways than one … but more about that later.

In order to leave the Emergency room, I had to sign a document stating that I was leaving at my own risk and against doctor's orders. I figured I had gotten by for so long, I could hold on for a couple more days before my husband arrived to take me to the hospital.

The first thing I noticed after being diagnosed with Multiple Myeloma was how easy the pain prescriptions came. Prior to my diagnosis, doctors had given me some prescriptions, although reluctantly. Whenever it comes to back pain it is easy to fake, and I realize there are people who take advantage of doctors for these kinds of prescriptions; however, I desperately needed them. The pain had gotten so bad that I could barely raise my arm to fill the coffee pot in the morning. I slept on a mountain of pillows because I could no longer sleep lying down or roll over as the pressure on my spine and ribs was excruciating. Somehow I was able to take my daughter to school in the mornings, make it to class and through the day, get home, take a pill, sit on the couch till it was time to pick up my daughter, get fast food and lie on the couch until it was time to go to bed. On weekends my daughter and I would stay in bed, me usually with a fever, while my daughter sat next to me on the bed playing her video games. Thank God for computers and games because without these distractions she would have gone nuts. By evening time, we would move to the couch where I would give her dinner and stay there until it was time to go to bed.

I was seeing a chiropractor at the time. She tried to adjust my back, but usually the pain only got worse. She could have easily broken my spine during those sessions. Once I knew what was wrong with me and I was strong enough, I started calling chiropractors and even made a YouTube video about my experiences. Since Multiple Myeloma is not something many doctors have heard of it is often misdiagnosed until it is in the later stages. I wanted to make chiropractors aware of the dangers of treating a person with Multiple Myeloma. The chiropractor who treated me for months, should have realized I was beyond the scope of her practice and referred me to get a CAT scan. Instead she kept treating me, regardless of the fact that I could barely move and roll over on her table.

One time I went to see an acupuncturist. In those days the pain was so bad I was usually crying when I went to see a doctor. It would be an accurate description that the pain had made me depressed by this time. That day was a particularly difficult day. When it was my turn to be seen I slowly got up and shuffled my way to the treatment room where the acupuncturist put a bunch of needles in my hand and told me to lie down. I could not do this without his help. When he put his hand under my back I screamed out in pain. He must have been right at T4, where my largest tumor was located. The pain was excruciating and those needles, as much as I wanted them to help, did absolutely nothing. He suggested I go see a specialist. This was just a few weeks prior to my trip to the Emergency room. I left the clinic in tears, depressed and scared. With all my knowledge about the body, I still felt helpless. I knew about the muscles and how to make my clients feel better, yet no amount of therapy and stretching was making me feel better. I was getting scared, but I had my little girl to take care of and school to finish, so I kept up a happy front for as long as I could.

I know the obvious question is: "Why did you allow this to go on for so long?!" There are two answers to that question. First, I didn't. About two weeks after the pain started to go from chronic to severe I went to a local Urgent care center. I asked if I could get a CAT scan. The physician on duty told me no. He said that insurance companies "frowned" upon such an expensive test. He did order x-rays which could not detect the tumors. I have often thought that if he would have only ordered the CAT scan I requested, the tumors would have been discovered and the treatment could have started months earlier without the cancer becoming so advanced.

Next, I went to see another doctor. One of the places that really hurt was behind my sternum, at the level of T3 and T4. By now I had also developed a bad cough with a constant low fever. A lot of Multiple Myeloma patients end up having lung issues due to a weakened immune system. When the doctor came in he asked me where it hurt. When I pointed to my sternum (close to my heart) he got upset and told me that if I pointed there he would have to send me to the ER to rule out a heart attack. Again he asked me where the pain was. I told him I did not know where else to point as that was where the majority of the pain was. I told him it was difficult to describe as the pain moved (apparently, wherever the Multiple Myeloma was eating my bones, I would feel severe pain). He told me he wanted me to pretend I was sitting in a court of law with him as my lawyer. He insisted I give him only yes or no answers. He was lucky that my word for the day was "patience", or he would have gotten a mouthful. I told him I simply could not answer him in that way. He said he already knew what was wrong with me before he walked into the room, based on the symptoms I had listed while sitting in the waiting room for over an hour. He told me I had asthma, gave me a prescription for an inhaler and sent me on my way.

I never filled the prescription, and have since thought of writing him a letter to let him know that the asthma he insisted I had was indeed late stage cancer. I am not one to go around suing doctors. I know they are only human and are, of course, capable of making mistakes. But with the way he treated me, other people likely would have benefited from my saying something about his demeaning bedside manner and his seriously wrong diagnosis. As the cancer was progressing I was losing weight and dealing with a constant low grade fever. I could not get rid of my cough and went to a lung specialist who did every test in the book, yet could not find anything wrong. One of the problems with medicine these days is doctors are so specialized that they only treat the part of the body in their field of expertise. We aren't body parts; we are human beings! Our body, mind and soul are all interconnected. By not looking at the whole person, many underlying causes of diseases can be overlooked.

Despite all that was going on, I stayed in school. It had cost me $12,000 and I was not about to give that up. The school I was going to made us clock in and out, and if we missed even just minutes, we'd have to make them up at the end of the semester before we could graduate. I could not financially afford this. I needed to go back to working as a massage therapist and colon hydrotherapist. I already had a couple of places with paying clients lined up and I needed to stay on schedule.

This was the second reason why I did not pursue the cause of my pain more diligently. Looking back, I cannot believe how I kept going, as a single mom and a student. One can either really appreciate what I did or see how foolish I was. I hope my readers will learn from my mistakes. Please, be persistent and get yourself checked out when you feel something is wrong! Do not take no for an answer! You know your body better than any doctor, and you know when something is wrong!

My primary doctor finally set up an appointment with a hematologist after one blood test came back showing I was severely anemic which explained the incredible fatigue I was dealing with. I had been anemic for years, possibly due to the Multiple Myeloma being present years before I was officially diagnosed. Because I was a vegetarian for seven years, I figured this was the reason for my anemia. Yet looking back, I realize I should have insisted on more tests years earlier, when I had a sense that my bones were frail. It is all water under the bridge now, but due to my mother's denial of any disease, I had no idea that cancer ran in my family. Recently two uncles passed away from cancer, and another died a couple of years ago from cancer as well. My grandmother passed away from pancreatic cancer, and my grandfather from liver cancer. I also had a cousin who died at the age of 39 from breast cancer. To top it all off my mother told me after I was diagnosed that she had a constant fever in her first trimester while pregnant with me. Her mother had died about six months prior, and Mom was a smoker throughout the pregnancy. All these things may have added to a physical disadvantage in my life. Add to that all the stress I felt in the first 40 plus years of my life, and one could argue that despite my healthy living habits at the time of my diagnosis, I was a likely candidate for something like cancer. Had I been aware of all this cancer in my family history, doctors (and I) might have looked a little more seriously at the possibility of cancer from the beginning.

My appointment was three weeks away at the end of November, but by this time my blood was turning to syrup with the plasma cells growing out of control, and it was hard for me to even climb the stairs to my apartment. If it wasn't for my friend Greg helping me every day I would have had to throw in the towel much sooner. We lived in the same apartment complex, and every morning he would come over to help take my school bags down the stairs and into my car. At school students would help take the bags with all my books and esthetic supplies out of the car. I will be forever grateful for the help I received during this period; I do not know what I would have done without the help of all those wonderful people.

The week before my diagnosis, I went back to the doctor and told him the pain was becoming unbearable and I felt absolutely miserable. He told me there was nothing he could do, I had to wait for my appointment with the hematologist. He told me if the pain became too much to bear I should go to the ER. I had started to feel so miserable with my fevers and the ongoing pain that I feared I might not wake up in the morning. I felt like I was dying and I probably was. I became deeply concerned about the consequence my passing would have on my daughter. I considered the possibility of her finding me dead one morning. How would that affect her life? At barely seven, what would she do? I couldn't prepare her for the "what ifs," that would scare the hell out of her! So the following Saturday I decided I could no longer wait. I had to go to the Emergency Room, and this time I would not leave until they found out what was wrong with me! My friend Greg and I dropped Naomi off at a friend's house, and so it was on a nice, warm and sunny day on the first Saturday in November 2012, that I was diagnosed with cancer.

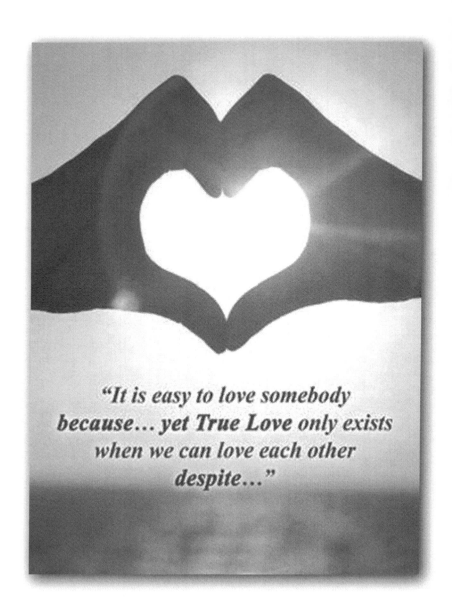

"It is easy to love somebody because... yet True Love only exists when we can love each other despite..."

3

Why My Daughter and I Moved to Arizona

*M*y husband Richard was on a mountain biking trip near Austin, Texas when I was at the ER. We were separated at the time. Naomi and I had moved away from our home in Texas to Patagonia, Arizona where I had gotten a job at a holistic healing center where people came from all over the world to be cured from diabetes through a rigorous three-week raw vegan retreat. I have seen many people get completely off their insulin within days showing that Type II Diabetes can be prevented and reversed through diet.

Richard and I had been married nine years and our marriage had been challenging to say the least. Neither one of us had great coping skills. When we'd disagree, Richard would respond with loud arguments, after which he would withdraw for days on end. Even though we had promised each other we would never divorce, I hated the way we argued all the time, especially around our daughter. It was *because* of my unhappy childhood that I figured a separation would be better for her than watching us fight all the time. As I had done so many times in the past, I reverted back to my coping skill of running away.

I know couples are not *supposed* to fight around their children. This is often easier said than done. My husband's schedule was the opposite of Naomi's and mine. He needed to get up very early and turned in at night before we would. This made it hard for us to have alone time as a couple. On top of that our daughter was and still is the kind of child who enjoys our company and did not like to be in her bedroom playing by herself, something I thoroughly enjoy to this day. When there were disagreements in our marriage that got heated, it was extremely hard to muster the self-control to stop the argument and wait until we could find the time to get a sitter and discuss the issues.

I loved my husband dearly, but we certainly had compatibility issues that often made our home less than peaceful. Coming from a childhood home where there was lots of disharmony, where I always felt I had to walk on eggshells because I had a mother who could be happy one moment and crazy mad the next, it was important for me to feel safe. An interesting fact is that most of my significant relationships have been with men that were very much like that, negative and short tempered. I read a book years ago which said that if we have serious issues with a parent we tend to gravitate towards the same kind of people when we are looking for a mate. The reason might be that we are unconsciously trying to fix the initial relationship by recreating the same situation in order to heal that part in us that is damaged and over which we had little control as a child. I can see now how that has been true in my life. My husband is a good man, a great provider and a wonderful father, but he and I look at the world quite differently. I am the eternal optimist and have a need to fill the energy around me with joy, Love and peace. My husband has pessimistic tendencies, is a problem solver who does not trust easily, and often criticizes. This had caused a lot of disharmony in our home and when I got the opportunity to get the job in Arizona, I took it. I told my husband I needed to do what was best for our daughter and me. I told him that the city we lived in in Texas was physically and spiritually draining me. With all the chemical companies around I did not feel good about the environment. The people were very kind, yet I never felt accepted for who I really was. I was this liberal, progressive woman with open spiritual ideas in a mostly conservative town that was religiously set in its ways. I have always embraced, even enjoyed people who do not think like me. After all, there is always something we can learn from each other. Unfortunately, it was made clear to me several times that the feeling was not mutual, that my thoughts were "wrong." It was hard to make close friends and, together with a house that did not see much joy, I simply needed to get away and recharge my batteries. Although this was hard on my husband, he agreed and has since realized it was one of the best things we could have done for our marriage.

At 5-years old, my daughter seemed to handle the move really well. That is, until we waved goodbye to her daddy at the airport in Tucson, Arizona. We went to the bank to open up a new account. She sat in the corner of the office and was quietly drawing. I realized I might have made a huge mistake when she handed me a sticky note with a heart drawn on it. The heart had a ragged line from top to bottom. It was a broken heart with two tears coming out of one of the eyes. She was crying like I had never seen her cry before and so was I, right in front of the bank clerk. I felt like a total jerk, like such a loser. How could I cause this little girl, who meant more to me than anything in the world, this much pain?! I did not want her to be raised in a house without harmony, where long nasty silences were even louder than the fights themselves. I did not want her to experience an unhappy home, something that had hurt me so much and had been so hard to overcome. Was she different?

Was leaving our home worse for her? I took her in my arms and asked her if she could please give us three months at our new place. I promised her that if she still wasn't happy in three months we would go back home. She agreed, and that was the only time I saw her un-happy about our move.

She did not share the extent of her pain until we moved back to Texas. One night she told me completely out of the blue, "Mommy, if you and Daddy ever want to get a divorce again I will not go with either one of you! Instead I will go out in the street so that I get run over by a car," she softly said. Her words devastated me. In that statement she made it very clear the impact our separation had made on her! Kids seem very resilient, yet we should not take advantage of this assumption, as often they hurt much more than they let on. I am not saying that divorce is never the better choice, because I know sometimes it is. Yet it's important to think about our children when things don't seem perfect in our mar-riage and not get divorced over small things, as happens so often in today's society.

Once Naomi and I got settled in our new home, I was happier than I had been in a very long time. Though my back was already hurting and I often worked more than 40 hours a week, I felt amazing. It was good to make a living. It was great to be appreciated for the knowledge I brought. The best thing was helping my clients, who came to heal their physical and emotional problems, through therapies and the ideas I had learned about life and Love, and the world in general. Because most clients' physical problems were due to living in excess, I told them, "A life well lived is a life lived in moderation. Except for one thing…. Love! Love with all your might! Love the sky, the moon and the stars! Love your children, each other, even your enemies!" It was here that I came to understand that we *cannot* forgive others until we can learn to forgive ourselves. We *cannot* stop ourselves from judging the world until we stop judging ourselves. And most importantly, we *cannot* Love and accept one another, until we can truly Love and accept ourselves. Though I knew I still had plenty of work to do on myself, many clients thought I was way ahead of the game. I believe this was because I was not afraid to open up about my own shortcomings, and my own health challenges. I shared my troubles and, in doing so, I was able to help others with theirs. Some called me "the Oprah" of colonics. The sad yet funny part was that I could relate with practically every issue, both physical and emotional, that my clients shared with me. I realized what a wreck I had been, yet at the same time I could see how far I had come.

The purpose of colon hydrotherapy is to cleanse the colon with a machine that has a tube that is connected to the colon. A slow, filtered flow of warm water goes in and out at a rate much gentler than an enema. For some people this goes fairly smooth and easy, but for some it is a real challenge. Our colon is like our second brain, there are a lot of emotions attached to the colon, hence the tightening of our stomach when we are nervous or the butterflies when we are in Love. I tell people there is a lot of truth to the saying: you are full of *shit*. The fact is, most people are.... literally.... full of it. This is not only due to our often lousy diets and lack of exercise, but it is also true for many people who have a hard time letting go of their past. I found that out by talking to clients who were unable to release, and by giving them a safe place to express themselves, they were able to successfully eliminate. It was amazing to watch a person start talking about the pains and sorrows in their lives and watch that pain being released through the colon. I know, for many, colonics are weird and gross, but having had my share of bowel issues, it has been some of the most rewarding work I have ever done.

I believe the best teachers are those that have been through the rough times, not merely read about them. I also believe that a good teacher doesn't preach. I do not believe in the saying, "Do as I say, not as I do." Why would any child listen to a parent who forbids things like alcohol, cigarettes, or drugs while doing these things him or herself? No, for me teaching can only be done successfully through application. Less preaching, more action, and willing to learn ourselves. Lessons are every-where, and they often come to us through our children. When we are open to listen to children, we can see how they, too, have so much to teach us. They can help us become our best, if we only let them.

It was in those months that I rediscovered myself. I found my self-esteem and my self-worth. In those months I got to be truly me! I made some wonderful friends and felt very much at home. Don't get me wrong. Life in this small town was tough. There was no daycare which made life with my daughter challenging, to say the least. I had to depend on Kindergarten and friends for her safety while I was at work, which often lasted past six o'clock in the evening. One of my jobs was to take care of an old-er lady. She was one of the most amazing and beautiful women I had met in my life. Bound to a wheelchair and her couch, living in an old trailer, there was not much for her to do. It was my job to clean out her bed pan, make her breakfast or dinner, and clean her kitchen and bath-room. Though I did not like being away from Naomi any longer than the 40 hours I already worked, she was a true pleasure to be around. Even with the severe pain from a leg whose femur seemed no longer attached to the hipbone, she was always happy and upbeat. If took her out in her wheelchair, she would notice all the little critters, the beautiful flowers, even the fluffy clouds. She was a real joy to be around, and she taught me a lot. I will cherish those moments with her forever.

I also saw how my approach to health and healing was a bit different from that of the center where I worked. I was more moderate. People would ask me if they could ever have cookies, coffee or wine again, as was strongly discouraged. "Of course you can," I would say, "Just do it in moderation, and truly love and appreciate that cup of coffee, that cookie or that glass of wine when you have it. Don't eat or drink with guilt. Guilt turns even the best of foods into poison, and adds pounds to your thighs," I would say, smiling. "Just try not to overdo it. But if you absolutely have to, go for it with gusto, enjoy every bite and know that tomorrow is a new day. Don't think of yourself as a failure for eating what you told yourself not to eat. Enjoy every bite of it, and start out fresh the next day!" People really appreciated that approach. From personal experience, I knew that when I had eaten from guilt, I could not truly enjoy the food because I felt like a failure for not having more willpower, and I would then just give up on my diet all together.

I thought I lived a very healthy life, and according to the standard set back home in Texas I certainly did. However, at the resort there were several instances where I was told that I did not live healthy at all. I lost too much weight when I became 100 percent vegan. I realized I had to eat more than just chia seeds, sprouts and avocados. I had been vegetarian for 7 years, mostly out of Love for animals. It was several months into my life in Arizona that I started to eat meat again. Why, you might ask, when I worked at a place that did not allow its employees to eat meat? For starters, it was a friend and coworker who already saw the anemia I was dealing with through the dark circles under my eyes. She suggested it would be good if I ate some free-range beef. Second, I realized how I did not like fanaticism of any kind, and I felt the restrictive attitude to be a bit too rigid. As with any place there was plenty of drama going on, which is fine. However, when somebody "caught" me eating yo-ghurt and told me I could be fired for doing so, while at the same time overlooking the infidelity that was going on at the main office, it made little sense to me. I also saw people coming in very sick and thin, and the solution to anybody's illness was always to fast more. How can an older patient, skinny to the bone from lung cancer, be expected to fast or merely eat a vegan diet? I had several patients like that, and realized that fasting was not always the answer.

I also observed that many people working there weren't really happy. Many were so very serious. I imagined spirituality to be a joyful affair; I know it certainly was for me. I also saw that some people, who did everything according to protocol, still had so many issues! In them I saw unresolved issues of anger, fear and sadness. At the same time, I noticed others who would eat meat or have a little wine on the weekends being much healthier because they enjoyed themselves and loved life. This is where I saw how important our minds are in the life we create. Joy is such a treasure of an emotion. I believe we came here to Love and to grow through the lessons life brings us. I decided I was going to start my own spa, and I wanted to go to school to become an esthetician. This way I could help make people beautiful on the inside as well as the outside!

During our time away in Arizona, my husband came to visit several times. Unfortunately, the visits usually ended up in arguments with me realizing I had made the right decision to leave. I did not accept any child support. My husband had told me I could not handle life on my own and I wanted to prove to both him and myself that I could. The separation was much harder on him, and he would lash out at me, even though we had both moved on and were in relationships with other people. Greg had shown up in my life on Thanksgiving and we had hit it off instantly. Although I was in no way looking for a relationship and was perfectly happy being single, one thing led to another and, before I knew it, we were dating.

Soon issues started to show up and it was at this time that I got to see how the problems weren't merely my husband's fault. You see, when we change relationships and the same issues follow us, we must take our own inventory and realize that the common denominator is us. This meant the problems that followed me were mine to fix. As difficult (for my ego) as it was to come to this realization, it was freeing as well. To know that I was part of the problem allowed me to work on the only person I could change... *me!* It is actually quite wonderful when we can admit our own issues because it is only when we dare do so that true healing and change can happen. Once we realize that we only have control over ourselves, we also get to see that happiness truly is an inside job. Though I knew I was a nice person, I had a need for everybody to be happy. I realized this was actually a very high demand. No one can be happy all the time, nor should it be expected of them. I often got disappointed if the other person was not energetic, smiley or happy like they were "supposed" to be. I also realized I was somewhat of a control freak, allowing myself to get upset over a bed that wasn't made or a person showing up later than they said they would. I am grateful I got to find these things out while we were separated as it has helped me with more than just my marriage. It is best not to have too many expectations of others, this way we don't set ourselves up for too many disappointments. I was willing to change the things about me that needed changing. I know I am not perfect by any means. Taking ownership of my issues rather than blaming another was quite humbling, it was also very liberating. This is a very powerful way in which we can make our world a better place. Like Michael Jackson's song "Man in the Mirror" so beautifully says, *If you want to make the world a better place, take a look at yourself and make that change!"*

Apparently my husband had discovered the same thing from his end. When he came by during the Christmas holidays in 2011 he seemed like a changed man. He had gotten his first tattoo at 54, lost weight, and started doing all the things he once loved to do. He had become much kinder and gentler to Naomi and me. I started to recognize the man I had fallen in love with. We celebrated New Year's Eve together and he asked me that night if there was a one in a million chance I would ever take him back (he knew I loved that line from the movie, Dumb and Dumber). Though I did not really think so, I said there might be a small chance. At that point I saw myself going it alone and being perfectly happy doing so.

That was all he needed to hear and from then on he did an amazing job pursuing me. By the following May he had won me back! When Richard came back to help Naomi and I move to Tempe, AZ to start my aesthetics program, he got on one knee to ask my hand in marriage … again. I happily said, "Yes!" However, I did tell him I was not sure if I wanted us to be living in the same house. I preferred that we have a LAT relationship (a popular phrase in Europe which means "Living Apart Together"). Although he was not too happy about it, he agreed. Neither one of us knew in that moment that by not getting divorced he saved my life. We were two weeks from signing divorce papers, something that would have left me without insurance. I went back to Richard because I love my crazy, silly, often moody husband, for better or worse, just as he has loved me in sickness and in health. It did seem like a cruel joke that after all we had gone through we got such a short time to rekindle our Love and had to go straight to the anxiety and uncertainty a couple faces when diagnosed with late stage Multiple Myeloma.

"If you can find a joke in life's worst circumstances, you have already won."

4

Going to the Hospital

The story about the day I got admitted is actually quite funny. It was Monday November 5th 2012. On that pleasant sunny morning we went back to see my regular doctor. It seemed the personnel in the office acted different, kinder somehow. Some staff had not always been the most empathetic, I am sure I must have seemed like a hypochondriac, especially since there appeared nothing wrong with me by looking at me from the outside. I am sure they were as shocked as I was that my diagnosis after all this time was cancer. The doctor told us I was to be admitted to the intensive care unit at Saint Joseph's Hospital in Phoenix. He had the floor and room number already available, and with that in hand we went to the hospital.

Walking had become a strain, and I had to go very slow. I was offered a wheelchair when we got to the hospital but I wanted to be tough, still refusing to accept what was happening to me, so I declined. We went to the front desk to ask where the intensive care unit was. A nice volunteer, assuming we were visitors, explained how to get there. I know my appearance did not give away the fact that I was the patient. With my thin body, which is considered healthy and preferable in today's society, and my forever smile, something I have always used to cover up the pain, people have often called me the "healthiest sick person they ever met".

When we exited the elevator at the ICU, there was a male nurse talking to a doctor. They both looked up surprised and asked if they could help us. "Yes," I said, "I am here to check in." Confused, the nurse asked what my name was, and after looking at his papers he said, "Indeed, we were waiting for you, but we expected you to be wheeled in! No patient on this floor has ever walked in!" Leave it to me, I always have to do things just a little bit differently. I had to undress and was put in a hospital gown. I got in bed, where the nurse inserted an IV in my arm and put leg sleeves on to prevent blood clots. Next, he immediately started to administer morphine. As the morphine entered my body my head got flushed almost to the point where I thought I would pass out, followed by an extreme warmth that enveloped me like a warm blanket and I felt much better almost instantly. Don't get me wrong, "better" is a relative term here. It made my pain bearable, at least while I lay still. With the pain deep in my bones, it still hurt like crazy to move, roll over or sit up, but somehow I was fine lying around for hours, dozing in and out. My husband was amazed at how well I handled the morphine. When awake, I was chatty and optimistic. My goofy sense of humor was very much intact and sometimes came out at the most inappropriate times, or so I was told. Because we had our 7-year old to take care of, my husband could not stay with me, and it was only with the help of our amazing friend Greg that we were able to get through the next couple of weeks.

Because my anemia was so severe, I immediately needed two units of blood. This was a first for me and it totally grossed me out. The nurse had to cover the bag and lines because seeing the blood go into me was a scary and nauseating thought. I must say how amazing I felt after those two bags of blood, how truly lifesaving this blood was for me, even if it did leave me feeling like Count Dracula. I felt energized and, between the blood and the morphine, I felt better than I had in months.

At this point the doctors did not know what type of cancer I had, so this was the start of six days and $60,000 worth of tests. I was not allowed to eat or drink anything because of the MRI they were going to do on me that day. More than 14 hours later, at 2:00 AM, they finally came to get me for the 2 ½ hour, full body MRI. I was thirsty, exhausted, hungry, and scared of what was to come. I had heard MRIs were extremely loud and, with all that had happened in the past 48 hours, it was something I was afraid I could not handle. The nurse gave me something to relax and, hopefully help me fall asleep. But with noise that sounded like I was in the middle of a battlefield full of machine guns, sleep was not going to happen. They gave me something to squeeze if it got too difficult so they could take me out and give me a break. I was not allowed to move... at all... for 2 ½ hours! That alone caused me serious anxiety as I am a wiggle worm. Somehow I made it through the MRI, which ended up lasting much longer because of the many breaks I had to take. When I was finally taken back to my room it was time to have breakfast.

Over the next couple of days there were many more tests, wherein every conceivable contrast enhancing fluid was pumped into my IV in order to better see what was going on. One CT scan was done with a radiation fluid that made my body glow like a Christmas tree and left me thinking that I was riddled with cancer because I could see my body light up on the overhead screen. A biopsy of one of the tumors was done, and I needed another blood transfusion. I loved the nurses and they liked me. I was a very easy patient and I spoke to them the way I had spoken to my clients at my previous job. Some of the nurses came by just to chat with me. None of them could believe how this could have happened to somebody like me. One of the nurses had a daughter Naomi's age and we cried together about how unfair this felt when you have a young child.

Life comes at us in strange ways and sometimes the most amazing lessons can come from the most horrible circumstances, but only if we let them. For me, after the necessary amount of grieving, cancer has taught me more in these past three years than all the lessons I have learned before that. Maybe I should state that differently. I had learned a lot of lessons prior to my diagnosis, but cancer allowed me to put these lessons into practice and that has been my saving grace, because what good is a lesson learned without application? To me it is like sitting on the couch watching an exercise class without participating, and expecting to lose weight.

The six-day stay at Saint Joseph's was like a honeymoon compared to what was to come. After a couple of days, they took me to a regular floor. After the biopsy, I met with the radiation team and an oncologist. This strange word Multiple Myeloma started to be spoken around me. I did not have a clue what kind of cancer it was. Like most people, I had never heard of it. The oncologist told me it was incurable, yet treatable, not exactly the answer I was looking for at 44 years old. They were contemplating surgery because one of the tumors was pressing inside the spinal canal and I could be paralyzed at any time. Even though the hospital had one of the top spinal surgeons in the country, it was decided that surgery would be too dangerous. Instead I would receive radiation.

Although radiation at the level of T4 proved brutal, I am grateful I did not need surgery. Radiation never sounded scary to me, it was not something I worried about. I was scheduled to receive 13 rounds. One treatment every day for two weeks except for Sundays and Thanksgiving. After that I would head back to Texas. My husband had gone home already: Somebody had to pay the bills! Greg stayed and took care of me. He took me to my radiation appointments every day. Because radiation is so precise they had to put three tattoo points on my body, one in the middle of my throat and one on each side of my upper body. Most daunting was the mask I had to wear in order to keep my head still (remember, I am not good at lying still and I have claustrophobia). The mask was made personally for me. In essence it was a piece of wax that was warmed and then put over my face. Once it started to cool down, while it was still on my face they put two holes for my eyes and one for my mouth. It felt and looked like a medieval torture device and I was truly horrified. Next I had to lie on a hard table with my painful back while they bolted the mask to the table to keep me from being able to move even just one millimeter. I was so scared!! What if I had an itchy nose!? What if I had to sneeze!?

The nurses were sympathetic but there was nothing they could do. The procedure would take anywhere from 15 minutes to half an hour, depending whether they also had to take pictures. After the first time I was given anti-anxiety medicine, which helped a little. The radiation oncologist told me I would start to get a sore throat after about a week. I felt great the first 5 or 6 days, then the pain started, and boy, did it hurt! I have never had a sore throat so bad that I could not even take a sip of water, never mind taking the medication I was on. Food, forget it! I was losing weight rapidly. I also started getting depressed. As the gentle fog of the morphine was wearing off, it left me with a serious bout of constipation. The severity of the situation started to become apparent to me and I became very scared. I was scared of the treatment. I was scared of the cancer. I was sick and tired of the pain. But what I was most afraid of was not being there for my children, especially my little girl who needed me so much. In all of this I felt the cancer was most unfair to her. First the separation and now cancer! What did she ever do to deserve this? I could not tell her the severity of my diagnosis, I could not tell her this was an incurable cancer and that her Mommy was in the later stages. She had heard about breast cancer and was afraid of it. Yet when I told her that I had Multiple Myeloma (not wanting to use the "C" word) she said, "Yes, but you are okay, because you don't have breast cancer, you just have back cancer." Sweet thing with her innocent childish mind. There was no way I was going to let her think it was more severe than breast cancer, when in fact I knew it was much worse.

Below are some statistics I found online from the American Cancer Association. These show that Multiple Myeloma is a very deadly cancer. In no way am I denying the pain and suffering that accompanies breast cancer or other cancers. I do wish to show how Multiple Myeloma is very dangerous and deserves much more awareness than it is currently getting.

In the United States, the lifetime risk of getting multiple myeloma is 1 in 143 (0.7%). In 2015 about 26,850 new cases will be diagnosed (14,090 in men and 12,760 in women). About 11,240 deaths are expected to occur (6,240 in men and 5,000 in women).

Breast cancer is the most common cancer among American women. About 1 in 8 (12%) women in the U.S. will develop invasive breast cancer during their lifetime. The American Cancer Society estimates about 231,840 new cases of invasive breast cancer will be diagnosed in women for 2015. About 60,290 new cases of carcinoma (CIS) will be diagnosed. CIS is non-invasive and is the earliest form of breast cancer. About 40,290 women will die from breast cancer in 2015.

This statistic shows that a woman with Multiple Myeloma (MM) has a 40 percent chance of dying from the disease, and that mortality rate goes up depending how far along and how aggressive the MM is. A woman with breast cancer has a 17 percent chance of succumbing to her cancer. As a stage III (there is no stage IV) MM case, my odds do not look great according to these statistics. I have never been someone who lives a statistically "normal" life. Had that been the case I likely would have died a long time ago. I believe there is a lot left for me to do, and I am not leaving until I am done!

Cherie Rineker

"Be brave and take on your problems! Pretending they don't exists does not make them go away!"

52

5

Brushing Things Under the Rug Simply Doesn't Work

Throughout my adult life my relationship with my parents has been difficult. I do believe both sides have tried and tried to make it work, yet the pain from the past has always been right there, ready to burst to the surface on a whim as it so often has. I thought that by talking about it, we could make amends. My parents wanted the opposite, brushing things under the rug. To me this is like covering up a dirty wound with a Band-Aid. You can do that with small cuts, but the open wounds we had needed to be treated and cleaned in order to heal.

I think in my mother's eyes I had betrayed her the most. Of all her daughters, I was the one with whom she was closest. Because I was a good child (this came from my parents' mouth), I had become her confidant at a very early age, something that had given me a lot more insight than any of my other siblings. I remember sitting with her in the bathroom while she was bathing my little brother; I must have been no older than nine or 10. She would confide all her disappointments and anger to me. She did not like the way she was treated by my grandmother and the rest of my father's family. She hated the behavior of my two older siblings. She even told me about my father and her and his demands on her. These aren't things a ten-year-old should hear, and they made me dislike all those people because I loved my mother so much. Later, after my grandma passed away, I found out how wonderful she was, how she had tried her best to stand up for us children. I discovered how much I liked my aunts and uncles. Yet as a young child I judged them based on the biased things my mother told me about them. My mother would always make me swear to never turn out like my two older siblings, which, of course, I promised.

It wasn't until I became a teenager that I started to see how demanding my mother's actions were and how she punished us by denying us love. She would literally put her hand at her heart and turn an imaginary key saying she had to lock us out of her heart in order to protect herself. My mother cried a lot, she was unhappy and felt unloved, yet she had no sympathy for other people's issues and was harsh in her words. I feel that she was not able to forgive me because in her mind I was the one who betrayed her: After all I had promised to be "good forever" and never hurt her. Today I realize I had a mother who used me to unload all her issues, issues a 10-year old shouldn't hear and couldn't fix. Then, when I needed her to be there for me during my teenage years, all she said was that I disappointed her because I turned out like my older sisters.

When I decided to move to Arizona I did not tell my parents. Though we still had somewhat of a relationship, it certainly wasn't the kind where we told each other much about our lives. It was more one of polite conversation without much substance. My father called and was upset because he had heard through the grapevine about my decision to leave my husband. All he could do was criticize me about my choice to leave. Despite the pain and conflict my husband and I were dealing with personally, Richard was aware enough of my parents' continued pattern of criticizing me and anything I did, that he called them and told them they should be proud of their daughter for once. He told them this was an incredible opportunity career-wise, that he was fine with my decision, and proud of my accomplishments. It silenced my dad and he told my husband he was indeed proud of me, something he was unable to tell me personally.

Because I was so happy and relaxed in Arizona, I was able to shed the pains of the past, including many of the deepest wounds concerning my parents. During that time, I enjoyed the contact we had. If there was anything that felt like my mother was trying to belittle or agitate me, I was able to brush it off, ignore the comment and let it go. A couple of weeks before Thanksgiving I received a letter from my father stating that they were flying to California to see my oldest sister over Thanksgiving. Although they would not be visiting me, Naomi and I were invited to visit them for the holidays. After my initial disappointment over the fact that they had yet to see their granddaughter even though they had visited my sister several times in the five years since Naomi's birth, I put the thought behind me and happily accepted the invitation.

The trip was going to require all my vacation time and two days driving each way. With my back slowly getting worse, this was not going to be easy, but I really wanted to see my parents and have them meet their granddaughter. I did not want to make the trip for merely a few days visit so I told them I would come for about five days. My mother said it would not make sense for me to get there that early as she would be tired from the trip and would need to rest. I responded saying it was okay, that my brother, his wife and their little girl could maybe go to Disney Land with Naomi and me. Immediately I received a letter from my father in which he wrote that this was *their* trip and that I was not to make the rules. He also reminded me of our past issues, issues they had told me again and again to let go of, and said five days would simply be too long for us to be together. Next, my oldest sister, who I had not spoken to in 10 years, e-mailed me a very impersonal letter about hotel arrangements. At this point I started to feel uncomfortable about many issues still surrounding my family and I. Even though I had conquered my past demons, they apparently had not. I contacted some friends I had in California and decided to make it a fun road trip of visiting friends, with a day spent celebrating Thanksgiving with my family. This, too, was not well received and criticized. In Patagonia I had been invited to several Thanksgiving dinners by my very kind and authentic friends. It was because of the awkward energy I was getting from my parents, as well as the loving energy coming from my local friends and family, that I decided to email my parents, thank them for their nice invitation and respectfully decline. Of course, this too did not go over well, yet I chose to continue the polite and kind emails and wished them a happy Thanksgiving. I heard from my sister in Europe that my parents were not happy with my change of plans and that I cost my sister money for the hotel reservation. To me it was a cause and effect situation and a result of their unwillingness to take part of the blame in how things turned out, and I put it behind me.

The emails from my dad stopped for a while, but by the time Naomi and I had moved to Tempe, Arizona they started up again. On top of that I was receiving written letters from my mother in the mail. Surprised, yet excited, I really appreciated them, including the pictures she sent along with the letters. I thought they, too, had finally moved on from our difficult past. Because my life was so very busy with school and Naomi, and because the anemia and bone pain were taking away any extra energy I had, I responded to my mother's letters by email. I wanted her to know I loved her and appreciated her letters as soon as they arrived. She wrote me three letters very close together, then they stopped as suddenly as they had started.

A few weeks later I received an email from my father telling me there was going to be a family reunion. He said that my younger sister could not make it, but the rest of the "bunch" could. He also told me that I was not invited yet did not give a reason! My heart sank to the ground. Again, I felt this hollow, deep pain, and the wound that I had so carefully treated got ripped right open again. Why!?!? How could this be possible!? Had I not let bygones be bygones as my parents insisted I do? What had I done wrong now!? Then it dawned on me. Could it be because of the letters my mother had written? I knew she did not like email. I knew both my mother and father felt the appropriate way of sending them letters was to take the time to sit down, write a hand written letter, go to the post office, buy stamps and mail it. Surely they had not expected that of me with my emails telling them how happy yet incredibly busy I was? As a retired couple with lots of time on their hands, hand written letters were an easier thing for my parents. Then it dawned on me that the letters my mother had sent me had been yet another test. A test I obviously failed, with as punishment my not being allowed to join our family reunion. I wished my father had not informed me of the reunion, but that was likely part of the punishment. It felt like salt being poured into the wound that I had worked to heal for so many years. A couple of months later my sister, Brenda (second oldest), came to visit me and told me it was indeed the disrespect my mother had felt from my writing mere emails instead of hand-written letters that left my daughter and I out of the reunion. At age 44 all the hard work I had done on forgiving my parents fell back to the wayside. I was devastated, hurt and angry! I also started to realize more and more that the issue was not me. Talk about expectations of one's children! Of course I knew that my mother never acknowledged her issues with me. The whole family knew that, but to deny me an invitation to my own family's reunion, therefore denying the family the opportunity to finally meet my daughter, their granddaughter, niece and cousin, was absolutely absurd!

This is what I mean when I say our wounds needed more attention than simply brushing them under the rug, not only for my sake, but for theirs as well. I was already feeling the effects of the tumors growing on my back and my spine crumbling. The emotional pain from my family was literally eating away at me. Could this physical deterioration possibly be a result of my lack of emotional support? As I am writing this, the question of why I got diagnosed with Multiple Myeloma is becoming clearer.

"Choosing to forgive someone who wasn't sorry was the most freeing thing I ever did!"

6

Saying Goodbye to My Best Friend

*E*ver since I was a little girl my sister Brenda, who was 15 months older than me, was my best and often only friend. Because my mother did not allow us much out of her sight, and we did not have many friends, we spent a lot of time together. As many older siblings could be, my sister was sometimes quite mean, but I would always go back to her. We did have a lot of good times together. When the problems really started in our house around age ten, because of our oldest sister Aimee's wild behavior we were there for each other.

My parents had decided to go out for the night when Aimee was about 13. She was put in charge of all us kids, but as soon as my parents left she was out the door. Later, we found out that she had gone into the woods close to our home and asked two teenage boys on motorcycles to have sex with her. Since her body had matured quite early, she told the young men she was 17, and they believed her. One of the guys felt weird about the whole situation and left, but the other one happily obliged. Of course, we called our parents when my sister did not return. They had to leave the party and were very angry. I was very young and did not quite understand what had happened. That night, whatever bit of peace I had known in my life was gone forever. There was a lot of yelling, and the next morning I saw my father cry for the first time in my life. I walked by the living room and saw my mother slamming my sister's head into the wall. I heard something about my sister needing a pill. Later I understood it had been the morning after pill. After that, Aimee was shipped off to boarding school for a year, and when she came back she ran away multiple times.

During a family vacation Aimee wanted to see her boyfriend, but my parents refused. The next thing I remember was my father on his back on the ground. People were standing around him and my sister sat on top of him. I heard yelling and the word knife coming from the crowd. It seemed my sister had threatened my father with a knife!? She took off and thankfully nobody got hurt. Brenda and I were scared, but we had each other for comfort. This was the last time Aimee ran away. At age 16 she got pregnant and married the father of her child.

My parents opposed the marriage because the young man did not belong to our "upper class." My parents often spoke of upper and lower class. I guess we belonged to the "upper class" due to my father's job as the president of an insurance company. More so, I believe the class system was very important to my mother, something she might have brought with her from Panama. We had to go to private schools, and we were not allowed to hang out with "lower class" kids. The sad thing was that even though we had to go to these private schools, where children wore nice clothes, went to sports activities such as field hockey and tennis, we were not allowed to do any of the same things. This meant we really looked and felt like the kids with whom we were not allowed to associate. On top of that we were only allowed to take a shower once a week and we were not allowed to brush our teeth. (I never found out the reason why, which felt so wrong especially since both my parents brushed theirs). If we were not respectful, my mother would punish us by denying us a shower for another week. You can imagine that this did not make us especially popular amongst our peers. I ended up resenting the "upper/lower" class scenario and when I ran away from home I actually felt much more at home with the people my parents did not allow me to hang out with.

At this time, I was still in good graces with my mother. Over the next couple of years, I listened to a lot of complaints from Brenda about our mother. I started to see how unreasonable my mother was and often sided with my sister. My mother was not kind in her punishments. Pretending to throw Brenda's radio system out the third floor window, something she had saved for with her own money, or ripping her favorite pair of pants in half, were punishments that were the result of her "attitude," something most teenagers struggle with as they find themselves in a body full of raging hormones. When my mother realized that we were talking about her, she no longer allowed us to be in each other's room. Life got really boring after that. By the time Brenda was 18, my mother could no longer handle her. Looking back, I find it very difficult to see a reason for this. Brenda was your typical teenager with an attitude, but in today's world parents would probably love to have the kind of teenagers we were. We did not drink or smoke, we did not have sex, didn't do drugs and were decent students. My grades had started slipping, which was due to all the drama in the house. I remember one of the last arguments my sister had with my mother. I have no idea what it was about, but my mother kicked my sister out of the house that day, and came to my room foaming at the mouth and collapsed. I was scared and had no clue what to do, but I definitely knew something was terribly wrong with my mother.

While I thought my sister was my best friend, I later found out that she was actually bad mouthing me at school. I thought she was popular. I was quiet, shy, and skinny, with a huge overbite. I thought she was cool and beautiful. When we were adults she admitted she was actually jealous of me and told lies about me because she wished she looked more like me. Jealousy is such an ugly emotion. It hurts both the person who feels it and the person at whom it is directed. I definitely believe that women can be each other's worst enemies. We need to stand up for each other, cheer each other on, and be happy for one another's accomplishments. Instead, we all too often stab each other in the back through nasty gossip and judgments.

When I lost my virginity my sister made sure she intercepted the calls from the young man. She told him I was not interested in him and that I was a slut. Of course, never hearing from him I felt horribly used. It wasn't until years later that she confessed this to me. As painful as it had been, I chose to forgive her and we moved passed the issues of our childhood. I would spend hours and hours on the phone with her, listening to her problems, helping her in any way I could. She was the kind of person you only heard from when she had issues. I knew when she was okay, because we'd lose contact. Even though I understood this, she was my sister and I loved her unconditionally.

About a month before I was diagnosed she came to America and visited me. I had warned her that I was in the middle of school and very busy. I wanted to see her but I did not have much to offer her, and on top of that I had my back issues. She said it did not matter, she just wanted to see me and hang out by the pool. We had not seen each other in years and I was super excited! We had a great first couple of days. She had just met another guy back home and was very much in Love. I was happy for her. My house was pretty messy because I simply had no energy to do anything besides go to school and take care of Naomi. My sister does not have children and is not very interested in them. This is fine, of course, but I was surprised in how little my sister cared about Naomi and how everything was about her. At one point I wanted to show her the things I was learning in school and she became quite agitated and asked if I could leave her alone.

Another unusual thing was all the times my parents were Skyping her. This was something I had always wanted to do with my parents, but they had told me they really did not like to Skype. However, it seemed Brenda got a call almost every night. She would excitedly tell me the next morning. I had to be honest with her and tell her that it hurt to hear about it, because they refused to talk to me. She knew that my father had told me I was not invited to the family reunion, and how much that had hurt me. I simply did not understand why she was bragging about them calling her. Later my mother told me it was my sister calling them. Was my sister doing this intentionally to make me jealous? Based on our past relationship it does not seem far-fetched.

One night I came home from school and was in a lot of pain. It was one of those days where I could not sit up and had to just lay in bed. It was Friday night and we were supposed to visit a friend of mine. My sister asked if we could still go, I told her to go ahead with Naomi without me, because I simply felt too bad. She did not show much sympathy but seemed rather annoyed. I asked her to please sit with me and grabbed her hand. I told her I felt I was very sick and asked her if she could please tell my parents that I loved them very much and that everything was okay between them and me as far as I was concerned. I was crying as I said this, but she let go of my hand and told me she could not do this. I had stood up for her so many times. Yet she could not do this one important thing at this very difficult time in my life. She got up and told Naomi that they would go visit my friend. Naomi came in to give me a hug and a kiss, and at almost seven asked me if there was anything she could get me. I asked for a glass of water and Brenda impatiently waited for Naomi to be done. Then they left for the evening.

My friend had a horse (Brenda's favorite animal) and she had offered to take Naomi and Brenda riding the next day. Brenda was all excited and took me aside to ask if it was okay if Naomi could stay home with me so that she would get more turns riding the horse. "After all," she said, "this is my vacation, and with you in school and sick my vacation is pretty much ruined." I could no longer hold in my frustration and told her what that sounded like to me. "You want your niece, who is also excited about riding that horse to stay here with me, while I am stuck on the couch because you want more *turns*?!" I always knew my sister was very self-absorbed, but this was just too much. My sister did not like the confrontation and after a couple of hours in her room she told me she was leaving a couple of days early. I think she missed her new boyfriend and was bored hanging around her sick sister. She told me it was going to cost her seven hundred and fifty dollars for the earlier flight, half expecting me to offer to pay. I told her if that was what she needed to do I could not stop her. I was physically exhausted and felt emotionally drained by her visit and selfishness.

My sister went to take a shower and I came in to give her a hug. She just stood there in the bathroom and asked me why I did not fight to have her stay longer. She told me how much it hurt her that I did not care enough about her to try and get her to stay. I told her how hurt I was by her wanting to run from me. Was it so horrible with us that she would rather pay $750 than spend one more day with us? I don't think she ever realized how that could be perceived as painful. We had one afternoon left and decided to make the best of it. We went to a wonderful place and saw incredible views and visited a nice little ghost town. Although I could hardly walk and was in a lot of pain, she did not seem to notice. Still, I was happy to leave on good terms.

There was very little contact after that. Even when I found out I had cancer and told her, she was hardly there for me. It was during this time that I realized that what I thought was a great relationship with my sister, never really existed at all. The last blow came months later when I somehow was invited into a Facebook conversation between her and a couple of her friends. One woman in particular was very rude to me. Obviously drunk, this woman started telling me what a bad daughter I was for not visiting my parents. She told me that her parents had died and how she wished she could have had one more moment with them. I reminded this woman that I had cancer and was in between stem cell transplants and unable to travel. She said that was just an excuse. In that moment I realized that while Brenda sent me the occasional nice email, she was badmouthing me yet again for not visiting my mother and father. These were parents who I had asked twice to come visit me after I found out about my MM diagnosis. Parents who continued to refuse, yet I was bad for not visiting them? It was the final straw for me. I lost all respect for Brenda and chose to end our relationship.

Since then my sister has tried to reach out casually, pretending nothing ever happened. I have chosen to keep her at arm's length. My life is much healthier and happier without her in it. I know she too is a product of our messed up childhood. We both simply handled the pain differently. I don't hold ill will toward her now, yet I do not care to put myself in a situation where I might get hurt again.

"Can we truly expect to get one hundred percent out of Life, Love or Trust if we are unwilling to give it all we've got?"

7

Moving Back to Texas

I had loved my time in Arizona. It was there that I found myself. I had grown so much and was genuinely happy despite the physical pain I had dealt with in the 16 months I was there. I had made decent money, bought nice furniture for our little apartment, and even managed to save and pay the $12,000 needed to go to SWINA, a holistic aesthetics school in Tempe, Arizona.

When my husband returned to bring me back to Texas the pain had not gotten better. In fact, it had gotten much worse. Not only did I have pain from the cancer, now I also had to deal with the many side effects the medication and radiation were giving me. I was put on every possible opioid to try and ease the pain. It seemed I finally found one that worked when I was given a Fentanyl patch, which was many times stronger than any of the other drugs I had tried so far. I put the patch on and was able to get a decent night's sleep. When I tried to get out of bed the next morning I stumbled and fell because

I was so dizzy. It felt like I had drunk a whole bottle of whiskey the night before and my room was spinning. I was nauseous and did nothing but lay around for the next couple of days. Though there was barely any pain, I discontinued using the patch. I was simply unable to function and I wanted to be present for my daughter.

Peter Schoeb, a wonderful friend, naturopath and chiropractor, who had been my teacher and mentor while I was studying massage, came to visit me almost every night. He would do gentle massage and energy work on me. I remember him holding my hand and us speaking of death as I felt I was close to it. I remember both of us trying to hold back our tears while I assured him I had no fear of dying. My only fear was that of leaving my daughter, who still needed me so very much. He did not say much but his wonderful energy gave me a lot of comfort. I asked him what I should do. We both believed more in natural, holistic therapies than we did in pharmaceuticals. Needless to say I was a bit surprised when he told me it would be wise to follow the advice of my doctors. His statement made me realize what my body was already telling me. I was seriously ill!

Neither one of us would have thought in those moments that he would make his transition before me. Sadly, on February 15, 2016, Peter passed away at the age of 62 of a heart aneurysm while working in Ecuador. He was one of the most kind and gentle souls I have ever met. He touched many people's lives as he had mine. Although I miss Peter deeply, I know from our heartfelt conversations that he was okay moving on when the time came.

My husband put my furniture on Craigslist without much luck. Thankfully the owner of the apartment complex allowed me to get out of my contract with a doctor's note. I had to leave the apartment as clean as I found it six months earlier and only had a couple of days in which to do it. Even with me being a minimalist, it was amazing how much I had accumulated in such a small time. We had to leave a couple of thousand dollars' worth of stuff behind, something the maintenance guys were very happy about. In return they allowed us to leave the apartment as it was. On our last day I remember sitting on the floor with the couch already gone, unable to move. My husband and Greg were taking loads of school work, paper work, and other things that were of meaning to me, and throwing them in the trash. With the weak state I was in I could care less, even though I watched my whole life being reduced to a suitcase and whatever could fit in a little Toyota Matrix. It is in moments like those, that we realize how little *stuff* is worth. Sure, I wish we could have gotten some money for the furniture, and I would have liked to have kept some of the hard work I had put into my six months at school. However, in comparison to what we were fighting for, my life, this was nothing. When I felt I was dying, the only thing that mattered to me was to be with the ones I loved. The more people we love, the richer our life is, and if those people love us back, our life is truly priceless! I can't remember all the details of those days and weeks; I am surprised I can remember them at all. All I remember about the flight home is that I needed a wheel chair, one I would need for the next three months. I also remember throwing up for the first time in years when we got to our home in Lake Jackson. It would be the first of many, and I had not even started Chemo yet!

A couple of days later we went to MD Anderson, one of the most famous cancer centers in the United States. People from all over the world come here in hopes of finding a cure for the many cancers being treated within those walls. The first time I went to MD Anderson I was in a wheel chair, feeling completely overwhelmed. I was scared to look at all the sick people and still could not believe I was one of them. As my husband pushed me through the many corridors, I saw people of all ages, races and nationalities. Some patients walked around with their chemo bags attached to a pole. A lot of people were old and very thin. It was at this time that I stopped looking at thin as healthy; instead I saw my own thinness and theirs as a sign of cancer. Being called skinny was never something I particularly enjoyed, but since my diagnosis I definitely think it is a word we need to stay away from as much as we don't call heavy people fat. We followed a woman into the elevator to the Myeloma and Lymphoma floor. She was all dressed in yellow, down to her shoes. She looked so happy and healthy. My husband and I filled out the paperwork and we sat in the waiting room. This beautiful lady must have seen my distress because she came over to me and told me that she had been just like me a decade earlier. She told me she had lost her hair more times than she could remember and almost did not make it a couple of times. Yet here she was, volunteering, happy and healthy. I cried while she held my hands. She was a true angel coming to me during one of my lowest times. I wish I knew her name so I could look her up today, and thank her for giving me the hope I so desperately needed that day.

When our nurse came to get me and saw me cry, she yelled at me in a thick Asian accent and told me to stop crying. She said that crying was not good for my health, and I had to be positive if I wanted to get better. I was way too weak and distressed to respond, though I believe she deserved a kick in the ass for saying that to me at that time, in that way! Of course I knew being anxious, scared to death and depressed was not good for my health, but how could I stop it!?! Again, I felt like a complete failure because I believed in the power of positive thinking! I believed thoughts were things and I believed in the power of affirmation, prayer and meditation! It was what I had been teaching my clients for years! Yet in those days all I could do was sit and cry while imagining myself succumbing to this terrible cancer in the most horrible and painful way. All the great things I had told people who were in distress, all the times I had cheered them on now did nothing for me. I had cancer, I was clinically depressed, and I felt like I was dying.

Looking back this battle with cancer has been the most humbling experience of my life. Never again will I tell others that they can control their feelings and that they can choose to *just* be positive. People give cancer patients such well-meaning advice. I believe that from the bottom of my heart. Friends feel helpless, and for some, giving advice is their only way of showing how much they care. But please, be cautious how you talk to the patient and what you say. Most of the time it is best to just be there for your friend or loved one. Check in with them and their family. Just listening can help so much. Take their lead! We are all so very different. Please don't tell a cancer patient to *just* be optimistic. It is very depressing to a patient who is in no shape to feel that way. That comes with time!! Yes, I have wanted to smack a couple of people with their well-meaning, *"just be positive"* advice. As for us cancer patients, we also need to realize how difficult it is to approach a person dealing with cancer. Many people don't know if they should say anything at all. It would be nice of us to not be too critical when people say things. When, in their well-meaning ignorance a person says something that might hurt, try to remember that the words spoken most likely come from Love and caring. For most people, cancer is still a scary word. We prefer not to say it. We call it the "C" word, like students in the Harry Potter series at Hogwarts who don't dare to speak of *"He who should not be named."*

Today, I still think we have a certain amount of control over our feelings when we are *aware* of them, but I no longer believe the control is all in our hands.

My oncologist was much respected. He had been working at MD Anderson as a Myeloma specialist for many decades and we believed we had the best doctor. We soon found out we were not a good match at all. He never looked at me, asked no questions, and instead started writing down my protocol without as much as a question. He needed the door of his office open because he was claustrophobic and his nurse (the one that had yelled at me earlier) would interrupt him continuously with questions about other patients. She talked very loudly, probably in order to make up for her lack in English. But no matter how loudly she spoke, I could not understand a word she was saying, something my nerves simply could not handle at that time. My husband and I both left very disappointed and I told him I would have to get a different doctor with a different nurse!

This is how Dr.R became my oncologist. He was a very kind and jovial guy with a passion for helping his patients get better. He took the time to call me before we met. Of course, I did nothing but cry. I could not speak to people in those days without crying. Later I found out it was not only the cancer and pain that caused my severe depression, it was also the side effects of the many medications I was on. Overnight I had gone from somebody who refused to take even an aspirin to someone who had to take about 11 different medications a day. Doctor R. never rushed me. I have sat in his office as long as 40 minutes. He always looks at me while listening, allowing me the time to ask all of my questions and concerns, and he was always very thorough with his answers. This humanistic approach is a nice and very rare trait with doctors as I came to understand. I told him from the start that quality was at least, if not more, important to me than quantity. I did not want to wither away slowly; I did not want to be kept alive at all cost. This was not how I wanted to be remembered. Besides, I did not have a lot of support at that time. I did not have a husband who knew how to deal emotionally with such a sick wife. I felt in the situation I was in; it would be better that I die than become a burden to anyone. Saying this does not come easy, especially considering how important it was for me to be alive for my daughter. Still I believed it would be easier for her to live with the wonderful memories we had made than to watch her mother suffer, unable to be there for her.

"Failure won't happen unless you decide to quit!"

8

Induction Therapy

My first cycle of chemo was brutal! Taking chemo on an already weakened body is gruesome. The Myeloma, out of control, with numbers in the 5,000 made me nauseous and my immune system extremely weak. My body hurt deep inside where the cancer was eating away at my bones. Now I had to take chemo drugs that would do the same thing?! At 5'8" and 124 pounds I was already thin, but over the next couple of months I lost another 14 pounds. One day I stepped into the shower and made the mistake of looking at my naked body in the mirror. It looked like the body of a concentration camp prisoner. I was horrified and would not look in the mirror again until I started gaining weight. I had a hard time taking showers and took them as little as possible. As a matter of fact, I had a hard time with pretty much everything in those days. Getting out of bed was excruciating. I could not sit up because of the rib pain, so I would roll myself off the bed on to my knees, keeping my back as straight as possible, then try and stand up. Thankfully, my legs were strong or I don't know how I could have done it. Sneezing was pretty much impossible and put me in a fetal position every time. I could not lean over the sink to wash my face or brush my teeth, as even leaning forward in the slightest would be incredibly painful to my fragile spine. I got out of breath just walking a few feet from the couch to the kitchen.

One day I was on my lap top and I saw my jugular vein protruding and beating fast in my neck. The Myeloma had turned my blood thick with Para protein and together with the anemia my heart had to pump extra hard to keep me going. My resting heart rate, which is naturally very low, was 94 beats per minute. I would try and talk and immediately be out of breath. I can only imagine how scary this time must have been for my husband and my daughter. Naomi was scared seeing her Mommy on the couch with a bucket next to her…just in case. As I dealt with fevers pretty much every day, often twice a day, and was told to go to the hospital when it went over 101 F, we would make that trip often. Though scary for my family, the fevers almost felt good to me. They made me lethargic and sleepy, which was the only time I did not have to be reminded of the nightmare in which I felt trapped.

I did not burden my daughter with my pains and worries. Even though it was not always easy, I always managed a smile for her, no matter how scared I was or how much pain I was in. My husband, though he loved me so, was not the best caretaker. From the moment I came back home and was stuck on the couch I had to listen to a lot of his frustrations. While we were separated he would visit us and I would see the kind and loving man I had fallen so deeply in love with 10 years earlier. Now, overwhelmed with work, shopping, cooking, and taking care of Naomi and me, the situation seemed to have become too much. He was coping by drinking too much too often. I started to feel that I had gotten back the husband I had left almost two years earlier, and I am sure this contributed to my depression. I did not want to burden him, but it was obvious that I did. All I could do was lie on the couch, apologize, and try to make light of situations that upset him. Our home was not exactly an emotional healing place for me during those days, but I had nowhere else to go.

Except for the sweet moments with my daughter, there was little joy in the house. Unable to escape the couch, I started reaching out to people online. I wanted to share my story. Some people deal best with cancer by not talking about it. That is not me. When my husband came to visit us in Tempe, Arizona for Naomi's seventh birthday in October 2012, I knew something was terribly wrong. I remember him and I going out for sushi. I told him I had started to think my symptoms were cancer. He got upset and would hear nothing of it. I told him I needed to be able to speak about these thoughts. I said that by keeping them locked up they felt like monsters playing havoc inside my brain. My husband told me he couldn't talk about it because he felt the exact opposite. For him speaking about cancer made it real. I asked him if he could please allow me this one thing – to speak about my pain and my body-, and I needed his support. He understood and agreed.

Sharing my feelings has always been an important way of communicating. I have found that when we share our little secrets, concerns or fears, we don't feel so alone. Facebook became a life saver. Not only did I have countless hours of entertainment while I was trapped on the couch or in my hospital bed, but it was often the only way I was able to communicate with others. When I was depressed and I could not be on the phone without crying, communicating through Facebook pictures was a great alternative. I was able to reconnect with a lot of people from my past. I found old neighbors and classmates who I had not been in touch with for over 30 years.

In 2013 I decided to leave something of meaning for my children. I did not want them to just know me as their mother. I wanted them to see me as the woman I had become. I wanted them to know what made me laugh and what made me cry. Because I did not know how much time I had left, and because I felt unsure if I would ever feel good enough to write a book, I decided to document as much as I could on Facebook. Yes, my Facebook page became a very personal place to visit. I talked about my good days and bad days. My posts showed the many passions I had. My love for spirituality, the right to use cannabis, and my political ideals. I also shared my love for animals and the planet and my desire for all people to just get along! Even though I am not an American citizen and I am unable to vote, one certainly would not think that by looking at my page. I mostly hoped to show my children that I cared deeply about humanity and the world. I loved deeply, and I had hope and faith in our humanity - if we could only practice what we preached by applying all the nice things we put on our walls.

One of the ways my oncologist monitored the Myeloma was by checking my urine. I would have to pee in a jar for 24 hours. The lab would analyze a protein called Bence Jones. People who don't have Myeloma don't have this protein, my number was over 5000. On one of our earliest trips to MDA, I realized I still had about 4 hours to go before I had collected my 24 hours. My husband and I had to hang around waiting for me to pee in the jar a couple more times. After my last bathroom trip I handed the jar to my husband. Apparently I had not put the lid on right. Half the content fell out onto his pants and into his shoe. He was yelling and swearing. I was weak and apologized again and again, unable to do anything else. We decided it was best not to tell the doctor.

When we got the results the following week, Dr.R seemed somewhat concerned with one of my markers, which had jumped up almost 1000 points. However, he high fived us and said the Bence Jones protein had dropped almost in half. We were super happy! Then I remembered the *"small accident"* and I told him how we had lost half of the collected urine. Dr. R frowned and said that it did make a *"bit"* of a difference. Thankfully we did not really understand all the Myeloma jargon and looking back, the fact that I dropped the urine is proba-bly one of the reasons I am still here today. Had I known the cancer had gotten worse instead of better after my first cycle I probably would have quit chemo. After all, both in my upbringing and in my profession of holistic therapies I believed that chemo kills. These first results would have confirmed my beliefs. Though my husband's foot got drowned in my urine, it is now a story we can both laugh at and be grateful for.

I had known from the beginning that a stem cell transplant was strongly suggested for Myeloma patients in order to lengthen their survival rates. I Googled what a stem cell transplant was. When I read that it meant high dose chemo and a 3-week hospital stay in which patients tended to lose a lot of weight, were often unable to eat for days due to severe nausea and terrible mouth sores, I thought I would not be able to do one. My initial attitude after my diagnosis was I would be one of those people that would only need a couple of months of chemotherapy and move on with their life. Although Dr. R told me I had quite a bit of disease (his nice way of saying I had a lot of Myeloma), he never let on how serious my situation really was. There was no way I was going to be the patient that needed one round of chemo, one stem cell transplant, and be in complete remission (CR). As I started to realize this, my depression and anxiety increased to levels barely manageable.

By the end of January, my body took a turn for the better. I still remember, clear as day, the first time I was able to sneeze without it hurting me. I felt a sneeze coming on and I braced myself to catch the inevitable pain and … nothing!! No pain!?! Unless you have dealt with this kind of torment for months on end you cannot understand how happy I was. I had found my first silver lining, the first of many more to come. Talk about enjoying the little things in life. I was ecstatic that I could sneeze without it bringing me to my knees. A couple of days later I went to the grocery store for the first time in months. I felt great! I had started to go outside and was able to walk to the end of my driveway. I no longer felt I would fall apart at every step and I joined Greg when he went to the store. However, by the time we got inside the building I was already worn out. I needed a cart just to keep my balance and any centenarian would have beaten me in a race down the aisle. Yet, this was the turning point towards my physical recovery. After eight months of excruciating back pain, rib pain, and exhaustion, my physical symptoms were finally becoming more manageable, as was the nausea. I was actually able to start eating again.

Two months into my chemotherapy, my oncologist realized I did not handle the combination of medicines well, nor was the caner responding much, and changed the cocktail. I was both nervous and hopeful about the new drugs. I liked the steroids because they gave me a bit of energy and helped with my nausea. What I did not know at the time was that steroids would prove to be a very bad drug for me, one that gave me suicidal fantasies. I realized I needed chemo, even my mentor and naturopath Dr. Peter Schoeb had told me so. I also believed chemo could kill, whether due to serious allergic reactions or a severely compromised immune system. Though chemo made me feel miserable I knew it would give me a chance at life. In a way, taking chemo was like volunteering to take poison because certain death seemed my only other option.

It was around this time that I was able to make a conscious decision to stop fighting that I had to take these drugs. I chose to stop looking at them as "bad." I refused to read the side effect labels anymore. Now, whenever I needed an infusion, I would imagine the medicine going through my arteries and veins like a tsunami, wiping out the cancer, leaving behind clean blood that allowed my healthy cells to take over and flourish again. I strongly believe it was my change in attitude that helped bring about my physical improvement. Once I mentally accepted the chemo I stopped suffering from the side effects as much as I had when I resisted taking them. I discovered that to fear anything is not very productive.

People are right to think their mind is powerful and capable of many amazing (and terrible) things. Yet when I talk to these same wonderful people they are horrified by the thought of using medication or doctors, therefore refusing to go for treatment that could alleviate their suffering. I know this because I was once one of them. I came to realize that this way of thinking could be just as negative. Being truly open to Universal Love is to let go of *all* fear. This includes the fear of cancer itself, oncology medicine and doctors.

I still had a long way to go, but I started to put the pieces of the *"mind puzzle"* together. I had read many uplifting stories about people miraculously being cured through affirmations, prayer, meditation, and positive thoughts. I was certainly doing all those things, yet I had not managed to beat the cancer that had invaded my body. At first it made me feel like a complete failure. I slowly started to realize there was an opportunity for growth in the way things were happening to me. How many people were in the same boat as I? Reading all the right books (including the Bible), doing all the right things (such as prayer), without getting the promised results. This was becoming very depressing to me, as I imagined it was for many others. I started to create my own philosophy concerning faith and life's bigger questions. I realized it had to do with *accepting everything in life as it came at me and being okay with it.* This did not mean I surrendered to the cancer. Far from it. I was determined to give it my best shot, yet I realized that what was most important was to live a good life.... *today*.... and leave the rest to the Universal Energy (God).

The reason I put the Bible, prayer and God in parenthesis is because I know these things are what so many people reach for, at least in Judeo Christian nations. It is not that I haven't or that I don't. What's different is the way I believe in these three things. In a sense I have been out casted by some for believing in God, Jesus and the Bible in the *"wrong"* way. This used to really bother me. I would try to persuade others to see things my way, or to at least accept me as one of them. Some have, others refused. This no longer matters to me. What is important to me is that I follow my heart and my conscience, and thinking that there is only one way to that special place is something I can no longer accept. This does not mean that I think others are wrong for believing the way they do. I simply no longer make it my business to be concerned about the way others think, and whether their way of thinking is right or wrong. To me, the world is much grayer than it is black or white. Trying to make a gray world either black or white is a very tiresome and frustrating affair indeed, and I no longer wish to play a part in that game. Loving others, just the way they are, is my motto now.

Of course, there are always consequences to our behaviors and thoughts, and for that we must take full responsibility. I can hear some of you thinking right now, "but

what about rape, murder, genocide, isn't that *wrong?!*"
It is my understanding that most of these things happen because people don't accept others just as they are,
and there are consequences attached to that kind of behavior. All I am saying is we are better off focusing on
self-improvement rather than pointing the finger at the
other guy, in which case we just do a lot of finger pointing without accomplishing much self-growth.

It was at this time too, that I started being able to take
small walks around the block. Every day I went out, I
would feel a little bit stronger. As I walked I would talk
to myself. I would think of every positive affirmation I
knew. I would talk out loud and listen. One day a thought
came to me; "When you are done with this journey, cancer will never be part of your life again!" I repeated this
thought over and over in my head and would say it out
loud, looking like a crazy lady talking to herself. I have
been saying it for three years now and I do (choose to)
believe that once this cancer is beat, neither I nor my
family will ever have to deal with it again. I don't know
whether my belief is true or not, and that is not really
the point. The fact that it makes me feel good is all that
matters!

I was told that the average patient goes through about
four to six rounds of induction chemotherapy in order to

bring the Multiple Myeloma to a manageable level before it can be attacked with a stem cell transplant. When I was first diagnosed, a bone marrow biopsy was done to find out what percentage of my bones had Myeloma. The test came back inconclusive. Another biopsy was done prior to my stem cell transplant. Before I found out the results I asked my oncologist what the preferable amount was. He said that although one percent or less was the most optimal, five percent would be good as well. After nine rounds of chemo the second biopsy came back showing 80 percent. This meant that my first biopsy likely had been close to one hundred percent. You can imagine my disappointment. Since one of the drugs had started to cause neuropathy (a painful condition that causes pain, numbing, and tingling of the peripheral nervous system, mostly affecting the hands and feet) and the steroids were giving me suicidal fantasies, we had to stop the treatments and move on with the transplant regardless of my unfavorable numbers.

In early spring I was hired for a part-time position at a little health food store in our home town in Texas. All I had to do was greet clients and show them where the supplements were. I loved my job, although I could only show up for three hours at a time. The manager had been impressed with my over qualified resume and even though it did not pay what I was used to, I was grateful for the distraction. I continued to be afraid of the upcoming stem cell transplant. Imagine your biggest possible fear; now imagine somebody telling you to do it or else you die a slow and agonizing death. This is how I felt. My fear was taking on a life of its own. I went to bed afraid and woke up afraid. I felt I simply could not go through with the transplant. Knowing I had no choice, I started to think of ways to get out of it. These thoughts became my suicidal fantasies. I saw myself taking all my pills and locking myself in the garage with the car exhaust running. I did not want to think these thoughts but they kept creeping in no matter what I was doing: watching television, reading to my daughter, driving to MD Anderson, these horrible thoughts never left me. I was so scared! It became harder and harder to meditate and pray. I could not concentrate. Every thought went to the darkest place possible. When I was in my car I started saying out loud everything I saw around me, in order to avoid that suicidal voice. "Car, tree, cloud, truck, person, building," etc. If I stopped for even a moment my thoughts would go back to my terrible ending and I would be crying like I had never cried before on that long road between MD Anderson and home.

At that time, I was seeing a psychiatrist. I loved her, she was very sweet. I would see her and cry. I was crying about my fear of my daughter growing up without a mother. I was crying because my husband was of little comfort to me during these dark hours since he could not handle the situation himself. I was crying because I had cancer, and because I was afraid to have the transplant. I was devastated that my parents refused to come see me and that my mother was telling me that I was not praying properly or surely the cancer would have been gone by now. She would always assure me that my thoughts were perfectly normal, and that every patient went through this.

Once I was on the list for my stem cell transplant, a social worker started checking in on me to see if I was mentally stable to go through with the procedure. I told her my fears and she assured me that it was ok, that everybody faced some of these fears. I started crying and told her about my suicidal fantasies and how they would not go away. Her tone changed in an instant and she sounded very concerned and told me these were definitely not *normal* thoughts. We hung up and the next thing I knew my nurse called and told me to get off the steroids immediately, and come to the hospital to see the psychiatrist the next day. When my husband came home that night I told him what I had done and he got angry with me. "Great, now they will take you to an insane asylum," he said. I cried and told him I did not care. I told him I wished they would. I told him this was too much for me to handle alone and I was glad I told them.

When I saw my psychiatrist the next day and I confessed the extent of my fears and depression she became very serious. She knew how much I loved my children, how being there for my daughter meant everything to me. I had told my psychiatrist that Naomi was my main reason for fighting this beast. She told me she had dealt with a lot of children whose parents had committed suicide and said, "Children of parents who have committed suicide never overcome that burden of guilt they automatically put on themselves. I know how much you love your daughter and your son, so put that idea out of your mind." I was both upset and relieved. There was no way I was going to do that to my children. But now I was stuck facing the stem cell transplant for better or worse.

After I was taken off the dexamethasone and put on antidepressants, my mood improved almost instantly. Later I realized how much I had stacked against me. I was dealing with early menopause, which the second cycle of chemotherapy had thrown me into. Most women have a hard time dealing with menopause all by itself. I was on strong pain medications, which can cause depression in and of themselves. Throw on top of all this an incurable cancer, lack of family support, and a deep concern that

I would not be around for my young child, and you can see how all this combined would put even the best of us on edge.

Looking back, it was no wonder I felt the way I did. Even though drugs are not the evil some people make them out to be, and may often be the difference between life or death, their side effects can be detrimental on so many levels and we need to be guided physically, emotionally and spiritually to keep the body and mind as strong as we can. Unfortunately, this kind of information did not come in my welcome package at the hospital. It is something I had to learn along the way. Diet, as hard as it can be when so many foods can make your stomach crawl, is very important. If you can't get yourself to eat, at least make sure you are getting the right vitamins and minerals by consuming green, organic, non-GMO plant based protein powders at the health food store. These are full of healthy nutrition and antioxidants. Exercise, even if it is walking to the mailbox and back, is very important. It keeps the lymph system going and works the joints. As my daughter knows intuitively, laughter makes us feel better. Whenever she gets upset or hurt, she goes straight to the computer and looks for funny videos. Appreciation is so very beneficial. I clearly remember the first time I was able to clean the toilet again. I mean, really clean, as in getting all the way behind the commode. Funny, but oh the joy that brought me. I learned to appreciate all the small things in life the way the old lady in Patagonia had. I can assure you, most of us have much more to be grateful for than we realize. Remember, I was ecstatic about sneezing without pain and scrubbing the toilet!! What are you grateful for today?

Many Multiple Myeloma patients I met on-line seemed to have an easier time getting into remission, but as I was becoming physically and emotionally stronger I noticed that I was better off in many other ways. I had long since given up my wheel chair and I was able to handle chemo better than many. I was even able to pick up some of my previous physical activities. Though I no longer could do strenuous yoga, I started teaching gentle yoga. I was also able to start biking and hiking again. I firmly believe that by keeping my body strong with a healthy diet, the necessary supplements, and keeping my mind busy by going to work and living a life with purpose, I was able to put a refreshing new face on cancer. I don't hide my diagnosis. By talking openly about cancer I hope to take the stigma off it. Most of us look at chemotherapy as a drug that kills both the cancer and the body. Chemo is not friendly to our good cells, but I certainly have found that we can keep the symptoms at bay through our attitude and lifestyle. Some people might think that talking about cancer is not the healthiest thing to do. I agree if it brings out fear. For me, after three years of dealing with cancer, it has become a way of life. I have to do chemo and go to doctor appointments, so pretending nothing is wrong is kind of silly. Instead I have taken cancer's power away by no longer fearing it.

"*Don't be afraid to try new things or think new thoughts. Many people will never fully live, because they were too scared to do that which their hearts longed for!*"

9

Getting Ready for the Stem Cell Transplant

*M*D Anderson assigned me a volunteer. Lisa, a wonderful young lady who had gone through a transplant a couple of months earlier, contacted me and during our many talks I got ready for the transplant that was to take place on August 26, 2013. She was so optimistic and upbeat about the whole thing. She was honest and told me the details of things I had feared. Yet in the way she spoke of them, I no longer felt alone in my journey and I started to realize that I could do this as well. All of a sudden I was getting impatient. I wanted to do the transplant and get it over with. I wanted to come out on the other side in remission and move on with my life!

The preparation for my transplant was pretty intense. After it was decided that I was now emotionally stable, we needed to determine that I was physically healthy enough to withstand the high dose chemo prior to the transplant. Thankfully, my healthy lifestyle came in handy here. I had done several triathlons and loved long distance running and cycling. My lungs were strong as a horse, or so I was told, and my heart was slightly larger than average due to my training. With the help of anti-depressants, anti-anxiety medication, counseling, and the support from my friends, I was in good spirits. Somehow I had survived the deepest and darkest hours of my life, both physically and emotionally. Now I felt there was nothing I could not do. My attitude had taken a complete turn. I felt like the old me again, the one I had become in Patagonia. I was even stronger than I was in Patagonia, because I now knew first hand that I could overcome pretty much anything. My biggest fear had previously been speaking in public. Now I felt I could do that without hesitation, and I had a deep desire to share my story.

I am the kind of person who will do just about anything once I put my mind to it. The truth was that I had not truly been committed to doing the stem cell transplant until that point. I kept hoping I would be one of the lucky ones who would go into remission without the help of a transplant. This hope was shattered the day I found out I still had 80 percent Myeloma in my bone marrow. With the autologous transplant, my own stem cells had to be used. I was given neupogen shots to multiply these cells to the point that they were pushed out of the marrow and into the blood where they could be harvested. For this I needed a Hickman central line, or a central venous catheter that was implanted to help with the administration of chemo and the other medications I would require. It was also used in the harvesting of my stem cells. This was no picnic. The shots caused my white blood cells to go through the roof, and I again experienced the bone pain I had lived with for so many months. Several days after I started my shots, my blood reached the optimum level for collection. My blood circulated through the apheresis machine, a process that lasted about five hours each day. My side effects included feeling extremely cold and sleepy as much of my blood was removed from my body during the procedure. I ended up with nine heated blankets on and around me, dozing in and out. It really was not a bad procedure. It only took me two days to harvest enough cells for two stem cell transplants, in case that would be necessary. Of course I had high hopes and renewed faith that one procedure would do the trick for me.

The day before I went into the hospital we invited a couple of friends over. After dinner my husband shaved my head. I knew I did not want to see all the hair fall out, something that was 100 percent guaranteed with this type of high dose chemo. By shaving my head, I took control and we all agreed I did not look too shabby with my new hairstyle.

The next day Richard, Naomi and I went to MD Anderson to get me settled for the next three weeks. There was not much to bring since I was going to be in pajamas all the time. During my whole stay I would be attached to bags of medicine and saline water. Nurses called the IV pole my *"stalker."* He was a complete pain in my butt. My *"stalker"* followed me everywhere, whether I had to go to the bathroom, sleep, take a shower or go for a walk, he would be right beside me. When it was time for Richard and Naomi to leave, we all shed a few tears and they promised they would try to visit in a few days. We lived about 50 minutes away from the hospital, so the trip was not impossible, but with my husband's work and Naomi's school, it would make it hard for them to see me during the week. Here I was, all by myself, waiting for my high dose chemo the next day. This procedure was supposed to wipe out the myeloma that had wreaked so much havoc in my life and in my body. Yet I was not ungrateful for the lessons it was continuing to teach me.

When the nurses brought in the bag of Melphalan, a drug that has been compared to Agent Orange used in the Vietnam War, I was surprised how small and harmless it looked. I had been told to start chewing ice an hour prior to the infusion to try and prevent mouth sores, one of the nastier side effects that would make it impossible for me to eat. I obediently chewed ice for the next two and a half hours, and to this day I cannot stand the thought of ice. I did not feel bad after the infusion, though this would change in the days ahead. It was highly recommended that stem cell patients get out of bed as much as possible and walk. We were supposed to walk the halls three times per day, do lung exercises to keep a pneumonia from settling in, and use the exercise bike in the hallway. I was determined to get through these weeks as healthy as possible, and I got up every morning to take a shower, no matter how bad I felt, followed by a walk down the hallways on the 18th floor at MD Anderson. At the nurse's station I would get a sticker with the amount of laps I had walked which I proudly displayed on my door. This showed the doctors and nurses that I was staying active. Many doors hardly had any stickers on them. On some days I had a chance to peak in and see doctors standing around a bed with a very sick person in it. The transplant was not easy on me; I can only imagine how hard it must have been for some of the older, less healthy patients. I spent a lot of time in those hallways, looking out of the windows, wishing I could be home with my husband and my daughter. It seems unfair how the fun times in life go by so quickly and the difficult times so slowly. There, it often felt like life stood still.

Two days after I received the Melphalan nurses came in with a bag full of bright pink liquid. These were my stem cells! These little guys were going to save my life. They had warned me of a strange odor that comes with the transplant, something like the odor of sweet corn. I never smelled it, though the nurses guaranteed me it was definitely coming out of my pores. The day I got my stem cells back was considered my second birthday. The nurses made a big deal about it, but to me it felt like just another day in the hospital. As my numbers started to drop, I started to feel worse and worse and needed a lot of medication to stay on top of my severe and constant nausea. Though it was no fun being in the hospital, it felt safe to be on the stem cell floor where I was monitored throughout the day and night in a place that was kept immaculately clean. With time going by slowly, and not having a lot of visitors, I made conversation with anyone who entered the room. This included anybody from doctors and nurses, to volunteers and the cleaning lady.

MD Anderson has an amazing volunteer program. There are more than one thousand wonderful people choosing to give their time and energy at this great hospital. They do everything from handing out newspapers and coffee to giving away wigs and scarfs. As they would come to visit me I could always count on a friendly chat. One-day Marc walked into my room and we ended up chatting for a long time. Though I can't really remember what we talked about, I do remember us both enjoying the conversation very much. We had a lot in common and talked about anything and everything. He left and promised to come back in a couple of days. The nausea cocktail I was taking at that time caused partial amnesia, which was a good thing because I do not really remember that much about the miserable way I felt during those days. When Marc came back a couple of days later I had completely forgotten about our previous meeting. I started chatting with this very nice man who I seemed to have so much in common with. It wasn't until the end of our conversation that I realized I had already spoken to him before and I asked him if we knew each other. As Marc later told me, he had no idea I did not remember him and was a bit disappointed when he found out I had forgotten all about him, especially since we had bonded so much over that first conversation. Of course, we laugh about it now, and have been great friends ever since. I had told him about my lack of family support and he invited Richard, Naomi and I to his family's Thanksgiving dinner a couple of months later. Ever since, this has become our Thanksgiving tradition. Marc and his wife, Twilight, have definitely been one of my favorite silver linings on my cancer journey. To this day, he comes to visit me every time I have to come in for an infusion and I never have to be alone in the hospital again.

On day nine I took a shower and I noticed my hair falling out.... EVERYWHERE!!! It was amazing how within the next couple of days all of my hair fell out, except for the hair on my arms and some of my eyebrows. This was a very interesting experience, and having shaved my legs almost every day since I was a teenager, it was a very welcoming break. I definitely count losing my hair as one of chemo's least horrible side effects, strange as it may sound coming from a woman. No shaving, haircuts, blow-drying or shampooing! My showers, which used to take at least 20 minutes, now just took a couple of minutes! Yes, I am aware this may sound strange to some women, but really, think about the freedom you gain when you don't have to worry about your hair!!!

By day twelve things took a turn for the better. Everyday my blood was drawn and while up to that point my numbers had gone to practically zero, they all of a sudden started to rise. My little stem cells had done their job and I was slowly getting better. When my numbers were near zero, I felt like absolute crap. It is hard to explain because I was in such a serious medical fog that I can't remember details. I do remember the nausea was unrelenting which made it impossible to eat; food would just come right back up again. It wasn't something I wanted to go through again! What was most interesting is how quickly my health improved once my numbers started coming up. From one day to the next I went from not being able to keep anything down to being hungry and having breakfast that morning.

I was released 15 days after I was admitted. I was supposed to stay close to the hospital (20 minutes or less), but due to the fact that my husband could not be in two places at once, my stem cell doctor allowed me to go home. I was so happy and though recovery would take many weeks it was great to have this adventure behind me.

My recovery was easier than expected, although it wasn't without bumps in the road. Initially the doctor wanted to see me every other day, but soon my numbers were stable enough that my doctor told me I only had to come in once per week. Marc told me he had never seen a patient recover so quickly. I was happy that I had only lost six pounds instead of the 20 I had heard of so often. Now it was a waiting game. It wouldn't be until around 100 days before I would find out if the transplant had worked and if I had gone into CR.

When the time came I had to go in for another bone marrow test. My husband was unable to make it to the appointment so Marc was there with me while we anxiously waited in the little room to hear the results. The doctor came in and hesitantly told me that my Bence

Jones was at 450. Because I was still in the thousands when I went in I was very happy. I grabbed Marc's hand and with tears in my eyes I squeezed it tight. I think my doctor was confused with my reaction because it definitely did not mean I was in CR. Right at that moment I was just happy that I was done with it, and that my number was less than 1,000. Next he told me the percentage of Myeloma left in my bone marrow. My heart sank when I heard I still had 30 percent left in my marrow. I had hoped for anything less than five percent, something my oncologist had wanted to see prior to the stem cell, but 30!!! How could this be possible? Right in that moment I told the doctor, "to hell with it, let's do another stem cell." My doctor looked at me in surprise. "Are you sure?" he asked. "Of all my patients you were the most scared, and now you are asking for seconds?" We couldn't help but laugh. Yes, I was sure, I wanted to be done with the Myeloma once and for all. If the first transplant was able to get me from 80 percent to 30, and my Bence Jones from 2000 to 450, then another transplant would surely bring me into complete remission. And so it was that on January 6, 2014, I had my 3rd birthday.

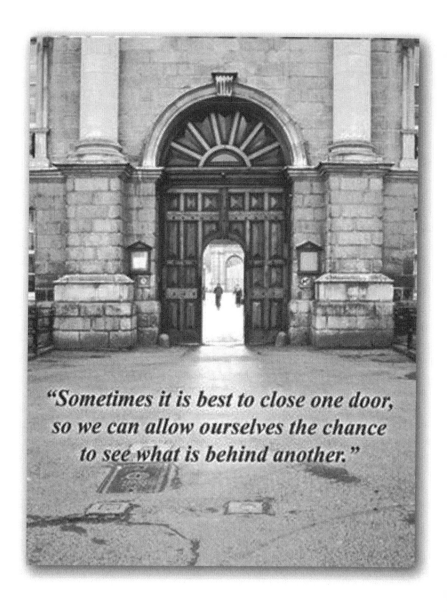

"Sometimes it is best to close one door, so we can allow ourselves the chance to see what is behind another."

10

The Final Straw

*M*y second stem cell was much more challenging than my first. My body knew what was about to happen, and as soon as I started chewing those ice chips I became severely nauseous. Our brain remembers things that make us sick very well. This is a good thing because it has kept our species alive by preventing us from going back to a food that made us sick or nauseous. For me it has been a very inconvenient evolutionary trait as there are many things I don't like to this day, especially ice, or anything I ate or smelled during my two transplants. Everything about the second transplant was harder. The motivation just wasn't what it had been during the first. The fact that I did not go into complete remission was probably a big factor. I walked less, showered less, spoke less. What I thought was only going to take about six months when diagnosed in November of 2012 was already more than a year, with no end in sight.

I had asked my parents if they could come and visit me during my second transplant. I heard so many friends who had their family around during their most difficult times and I wanted this, too. My oldest sister had needed surgery years' prior in California, and both my parents had jumped on a plane to be there for her. I hoped and prayed that they would do the same for me. My father had taught me it was always better to ask, so I decided to ask them one more time. He told me that coming for a visit while I was in the hospital made little sense, but that they would talk about coming over in the spring when I was on the mend. It was better than nothing and I was happy and hopeful about seeing them.

My stay at MD Anderson during my second transplant was only a couple of days more than it had been the first time, and again I recuperated really fast. I went back to work at my little health food store about one month after I came home from the hospital. Still pretty much bald, yet in good spirits and hopeful, I heard I was an inspiration to the clients that came to our store. Life went on as usual but I was anxiously waiting for the results of my second stem cell with great hopes of CR. Three months after I was released from the hospital, I went to my doctor's appointment to find out the results. This time the news was even more discouraging. Although my numbers had gone down, they had not made a drastic drop; as a matter of fact, there were several cycles during my initial therapy where my numbers had dropped much more significantly than they had with my second transplant. I was very disappointed. My stem cell doctor wanted to do another bone marrow biopsy but I refused. What was the point? I could not handle finding out that it was still no less than five percent. Gone were the days of high expectations. I asked my stem cell doctor what my next step was. He told me I would likely be on maintenance therapy indefinitely. "Can I do a third transplant," I asked him hesitantly. "No," he said. "Studies have not shown much improvement with a third transplant, your next option will be an "allo" or donor transplant. I had heard that allogenic transplants were much riskier, especially for Multiple Myeloma patients, and the results were often disappointing. I had followed a guy with Multiple Myeloma, whose wife kept a blog on-line. After two autos and one allo transplant he had died from GVHD (graft-versus-host-disease) complications. It seemed that with an allo transplant, I could be stuck with two types of terrorists in my body, the MM and the GVHD, an immune response which can cause serious, potentially life-threatening complications such as irreversible organ damage. Quality being my most important goal, I decided to pass on this treatment.

119

Foolishly I had hoped that my diagnosis would bring me closer to my parents. Things did seem better initially, but soon I realized that my parents were very uncomfortable dealing with me and my cancer diagnosis. After all, my mother was a Christian Scientist and was completely against the use of doctors and medicine of any kind. My father seemed just plain uncomfortable dealing with any illness. My mother started to pray for me and suggested I start reading '*Science and Health with Key to the Scriptures*' by Mary Baker Eddy, founder of Christian Science. When she found I was not getting better she got frustrated and started hinting that I was not being faithful enough. She made me feel like I was praying wrong. I think prayer is fantastic, yet I have seen too many wonderful people that were loyal in their faith and prayers, lose their battles with cancer. For many patients it seems all the faith in the world won't help. I had cancer and needed help beyond faith and prayer. Because of my mother's interpretation of faith, God and religion no longer made as much sense to me as I wished it did.

About a month before I went into the hospital for my transplant, my father called and told me that he and my mother were sick. He told me not to worry, not to pray and that they had everything under control. The fact that they did not want me to pray felt weird but I respected their wishes. You can imagine my surprise when I got an e-mail from one of my aunts saying that my parents were sick and being treated by a physician. Needless to say I was upset because it seemed that though I should be able to heal myself from *cancer* with prayer, my parents could get medical help for bronchitis!? When I spoke to my mother a while later I could not help but let her know that I heard she and Dad had been treated for their illness. "Well, you know, when people around us were wanting us to go the medical route, their fear was too strong for my prayers to work," she told me. Flabbergasted, I responded, "Can you just imagine the amount of negative, fearful energy I have had to deal with when people found out I had cancer! Can you see how maybe I was unable to go up against that too!?" Of course my mother did not see her hypocrisy and I left it at that.

For the sake of understanding the dysfunction between my mother and me, I have chosen to add a couple more incidences about my life. In much of my life I have had close friends, both my husbands, and even my own son ask me why I did not simply kick my parents out of my life and move on. Looking back, I probably should have, but my honest answer has been that I simply love my parents and longed to have a "*normal*" and respectful relationship with them. I have never stopped loving my mother and I felt an incredible need to be accepted by her for who I was and get back in her heart. We only have one biological mother and father, and it is widely known that many children will go to great lengths to try and get love and approval from their parents well into adulthood. Since I had cut my own childhood short by running away, I was still longing for that approval in a very childlike manner.

After I ran away from home it was years before my mother and I were able to have anything resembling a normal relationship. I became a flight attendant in 1995 and by 1997 I was flying international and had a lot of Heathrow layovers. I was dating a pilot, something my parents approved of, and I spent a lot of time at my parents' home during layovers. I was happy! My mother and I could talk for hours, yet after a while thing would come up and the pain of the past would resurface on both sides. I also started to realize how little I really had in common with my parents. My values were so different from theirs. I am open to all kinds of people, beliefs and behaviors. As long as it does not hurt anybody or anything, I am fine with the choices other people make. I feel it is none of my business anyway. My parents have built a very safe wall around them, only letting people in that abide by their values.

My relationship with Paul the pilot lasted five years. They were some of the best years of my life. I had wanted to become a "stewardess" since I was a little girl, hoping to live a "fairy-tale" life by flying to exotic places all over the world. With Paul as my captain I felt I was experiencing that dream. I don't regret a minute of our relationship. He taught me so much about who I was and what I wanted in life. Paul was an amazing father of three beautiful children. In my eyes he spoiled them too much, but those were the eyes of a child that had not seen unconditional love from her own parents. I could not fathom the amount of sacrifices he made, even at the expense of our relationship. In the way I was raised, my mother always said that children came last. She told me on many occasions that my time would come. Here I was, in love with a man who made it quite clear to me that his children came first. This just did not sit well with me at the time. When was it going to be my turn!

It is interesting to see how those of us who have lived through difficult childhoods get jealous when we see other children living the kind of childhood we wished we'd had. I have recognized it in quite a few other people besides myself, especially women who do not have children themselves. Thankfully the birth of my daughter changed the way I look at this. She has been the opportunity for me to give those things I and every child deserves: Love, safety, patience, respect and positive attention, among many other things. Though I never had a soft place to fall, I have become my daughter's soft place, and this has fulfilled me and helped me heal from the traumas of my own childhood.

Though my Love for Paul was real, our relationship came to an end due to my inner demons and some of his behaviors. A few months later I met my future husband Richard. When my son and I visited my parents over Christmas and New Year, I told them about the new man in my life. I asked my father to please put away the picture of Paul and me that was displayed on the piano. My mother came out of the kitchen and refused. Again, she was showing me that my feelings in no way mattered to her. I was now 34 years old, but I still felt like that 17-year old girl that had run away from home.

Everything went reasonably well until my son tried to get a pebble out of his shoe. My mother jumped up and started yelling at him for making a mess. I became momma bear and told my mother to take it easy, that Michael was simply trying to take a pebble out of his shoe. My mother completely lost it (obviously this was years of anger coming out), and told me to go to my room. I got up and she followed me. When I opened the door to leave she raised her hand to hit me. I grabbed her arm and told her she would never hit me again. I stepped out into the hallway and slammed the door behind me. I was furious, it was New Year's Eve and I could not get out of there soon enough. An hour or so later my son came down and begged me to come up so that we could all celebrate the New Year. I told him I simply couldn't. He begged me to please do it for him. He also told me that the only way I was allowed to come up was to apologize to my parents. I told him I was only protecting him and that I had nothing to apologize for. He asked me to please do so for him, and so I went back up to my parents' apartment and stood in front of them like a child that could do no right in my parents' eyes and apologized over nothing at all.

Of course, that night was extremely tense and the next day my son and I went back to America. My parents and I did not talk after that. Like so many times before, we were both too upset to make up. When Richard and I got married a couple of months later, we did not tell anybody, including my parents, something that deeply disturbed them. The interesting thing is how they always got upset at my behavior without ever taking ownership as to why I made the decisions I did. Today, I am sure

I would have handled many situations better. Today I could just let things go and not take them so seriously. But then, just like my mother, I was full of pent up anger and hurt.

After I had heard about my parents' medical help, while refusing to acknowledge that I might need help as well in treating cancer, I further distanced myself from them. I was not rude when they called, but I was not going out of my way to contact them anymore. Then, one day, months after my second transplant, well past the spring when my father had promised me he would consider visiting, my mother called me out of the blue. I took the phone and went outside to sit by the pool in order not to disturb my husband with our conversation. Pretty much instantly she told me how she had read a certain article about how cancer patients are such a great burden on society. She then told me we really needed to let cancer patients die. I could not believe my ears! I felt like hanging up the phone but instead I said very calmly, "You know Mom that would mean that your granddaughter would be raised without a mother." "Stop that nonsense," she hissed, "You don't have cancer!" I don't know why I did not hang up right then, but somehow I made it through the call. As she continued to belittle me and told me how I had to stop being so negative, I could not help but suggest she pick up the dictionary and look up the word "projection". She was quiet after that and I wished her a happy day. I got off the phone feeling devastated and angry. I told my husband, who, after listening to me crying about my parents for 12 years was tired of the whole story. He suggested I just forget about them and move on with my life.

Thankfully I had an appointment with my psychiatrist the following week. I told her what my mother had said and how it had completely devastated me. "Cherie," she started, "You have done everything you can to salvage this very fragile relationship. It seems your mother is doing everything she can to keep you away. Though this is not the advice I usually give my patients, I will tell you that it is okay to let her go and be free of the heartache she continues to cause." I knew instantly that she was right. I knew it was what I needed to hear. It was her professional opinion that finally allowed me to let go of the relationship. It felt like 40 years' worth of weight was lifted off my shoulders. It was in that moment, too, that I realized I was not angry or sad anymore. I felt pity for a woman who had missed an opportunity to have a relationship with her daughter and wonderful granddaughter. For the first time I felt the loss was not mine but hers.

I did not let go of my relationship with my father at that time, though I knew it would be difficult to communicate with one parent and not the other. I did not contact him but was cordial if he called. My relationship with him ended a couple of months later when I got another e-mail which stated that the family had celebrated yet another wonderful reunion, where *"everybody"* had shown up. Obviously, I wasn't counted as "everybody" in the family and again I had not received an invitation. He said how happy *everybody* was to see each other again and that it was sad to see *everybody* go. I remember the emphasis on the word *everybody* and again I had that hollow feeling in the gut of my stomach. Fortunately, I was able to see in that moment that I wasn't the one with the problem and that my life would be a lot better off without this kind of harassment. I forgave them in that instant and have not regretted my decision since. As a matter of fact, once the burden of trying to please them was gone, I was able to truly be me. Finally, at the age of 46 I had grown up. My life became happier than it had ever been. I was able to become my authentic self. Self-esteem was no longer something I only read about. I started to accept and like me for who I was, flaws and all, for the first time in my life! This showed me that for me being sick physically hurt a lot less than being emotionally injured. This "goodbye" to my parents opened up my life to welcome in all kinds of wonderful people.

I had always kept my heart somewhat shut because all I ever wanted was my parents' Love and acceptance. Now I no longer needed that. Instead, I gave Love and acceptance to all I touched and felt that Love returned many times over.

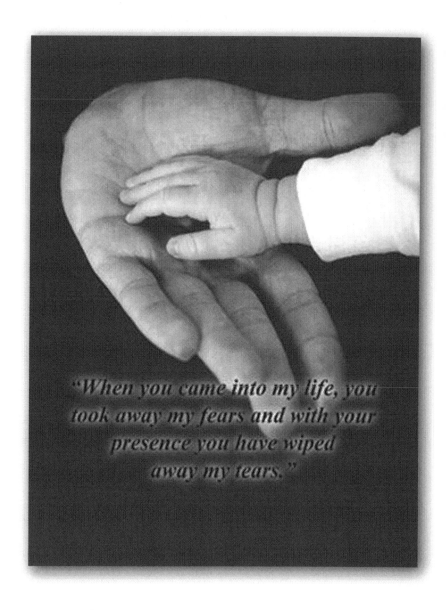

"When you came into my life, you took away my fears and with your presence you have wiped away my tears."

11

Naomi, a Gift From Heaven

*B*efore I start this chapter, I want to make it very clear that I love both my children equally. They were both wanted and I have loved them with every ounce of my being. When Michael went to live with his father at age five I tried everything I could to stay in touch with him, but with him living in Massachusetts and me in Texas, this has not always been easy. The love I feel for him runs deep, yet with our physical distance it is impossible to have the same kind of relationship I have with my daughter. Though this chapter is about her, the Love for my son needs to be expressed!

As I had stated in the beginning of my book, my daughter, Naomi, saved my life in more ways than one. Being more familiar with the challenges I have faced, I hope the reader can understand what an incredible blessing my daughter has been in my life.

The interesting thing is that I never wanted a daughter. When I was pregnant with my son, I was scared to be carrying a girl, scared that I would become the same kind of mother to a daughter as my mother had been to me. My mother told me that girls were extremely difficult, and she clearly enjoyed my brother a lot more. I believed her during that time, and feared I would not be able to handle a girl. I felt extremely relieved when it turned out that I was going to have a son. When I had to give him up at the age of five, I felt I wasn't a good mother and did not deserve to have any more children. Although I was only in my 20's I was not interested in starting a new family.

When Richard and I met, neither one of us had a particular need to become parents. He and his ex-wife had tried for years without luck, so I figured children would not be part of the picture and that was fine with me. We decided we would just enjoy each other and leave the rest up to God. We were in our first year of marriage when all that changed. On a nice sunny day, I was in the bathroom and my husband walked by. At that moment I knew I was ready for a girl and I told him. The thought came out of nowhere. I had been doing a lot of soul searching and I felt I had worked through most of my childhood issues. The next month my husband had to go to Germany for work. Around that time, I had a dream in which an angel came to me and told me I was going to have a baby girl. I was to name her Naomi Nicole. I remember waking up happy and surprised yet not making much of the dream.

My husband was in Germany for about a week when I noticed my breasts getting sore. This happened only when I was pregnant so I went to the store and bought a pregnancy test. It came back negative and I was somewhat disappointed. Over the next couple of days, I continued to feel the sensitivity in my breasts and again I went to the store to buy a test. I did not want to wait till I got home so I went into the store bathroom, peed on the stick and as I walked to the front of the store to pay for the empty box I was staring at the window where very slowly one line started to show up. The lady at the cash register kind of shook her head as she accepted my money, but I did not care. One line had shown up; I was not pregnant. This time I was really disappointed. I got into my car and started driving, occasionally looking at the stick. Very vaguely a second line started to appear and my heart skipped a beat. By the time I arrived home there was a definite second line and I felt ecstatic.

I had nobody to tell as my husband was in Europe. Richard was 47 years old and had never had a child. We had enjoyed our time together alone. Since he told me it was okay not to have a child I was not sure if he would be excited about the news and I got nervous. I called him in Germany and he was very happy to hear from me. I did not know how to tell him so I told him I had news yet wasn't sure if it was good or bad. He got all nervous and agitated and told me to just spit it out. I said, "Well, honey, we are pregnant." There was a long pause on the other side, then he said, "And what is bad about that." I let out a big sigh and started laughing. He was both upset and laughing about the horrible way I brought him the news.

We were both extremely proud and excited and I cherished the next nine months to the fullest. Still nervous about how to raise a child I bought every book I could find about parenting and watched Nanny 911 religiously. I did not want to screw up again. We chose not to find out about the sex of the baby, though by week 30 I could no longer contain my curiosity and we went to a place that did 3D baby pictures. My son was with us and while he hoped for a little brother (he was 15 at the time) my secret prayer was for a girl. It took a while for the technician to get the baby in the right position, then she asked if we wanted to know what it was. YES, PLEASE!!! "Congratulations, you are going to be the proud parents of a baby girl," she said. I let out a cry of happiness and looked over to see my son. He looked happy for me. "Hey, as long as she is healthy," he said. What a guy!!

The birth was beautiful. A dear friend of mine came to the house weeks prior to do Reiki on me and Naomi. Several times she was hiccupping and it was always amazing to feel her relax when Shay, my friend and Doula, would put her hands on my belly. The hiccups would stop instantly.

Naomi came into the world seven days before her due date. My belly had stopped growing and was actually getting smaller. The doctor was concerned and ordered me into the hospital the next day. She stripped my membranes in hopes of getting the delivery started and said she would induce the next day, if necessary. That night I was very uncomfortable. I had many contractions though they were far apart. Unable to sleep I knew how much our lives would change and I was a bit concerned about Richard. Although I had told him how children changed a relationship, he did not really seem to believe me. He thought you fed a baby, changed diapers and walked them (like a dog). I told him that was the easy part. "It is the time in between when they are awake and you have no clue what to do with them that is the challenge," I would tell him. He did not believe me but was soon to find out! The next morning, we got a very early call from the hospital. They said that we could not come in. The pregnancy ward was full and we would have to wait another day. Disappointed and tired I decided to take a bath. The last three weeks had been hard. I have a uterus that tips inward. This means I hide my pregnancies well, but it also means it presses against all my organs. My kidneys had been hurting and most of my time was spent hanging over a big exercise ball trying to relieve the pressure. When I got out of the bathtub my water broke. The next contraction hit hard and brought me to my knees. At that moment my husband came back from walking our dog and found me at the top of the stairs gripping onto the railing, panting "We have to go to the hospital." "We can't," he said, "They don't have room." "Tell them they are going to have to make room," I hissed, "My water just broke!!" We called the hospital and the lady reminded us that they told us we could not come because they had no rooms. My husband explained that my water had broken and the lady told us to come in, that the hospital kept an "extra" room for emergencies like these.

We had decided on natural birth. I really wanted a home birth, but the nearest midwife lived an hour away and wanted to charge $2,000, which our insurance would not reimburse. I decided I did not need a home birth that badly, and we got an obstetrician who was very open to our desire to have Naomi as natural as possible. Shay would be with us as my doula and it would be an intimate affair. When we got to the hospital and I had to sign in the lady paused, looked at me and asked, "So who is having the baby?" As I said I did not show much, as a matter of fact, my breasts were still bigger than my belly, and I had only gained 19 pounds, so with certain clothes people could not see that I was pregnant. I was just in between a contraction and smiling; I said, "I am."

When we got to our floor every door had a sign on it saying epidural. Apparently I was the only one who decided to give birth naturally. Although I did believe going the natural way would be good for my baby, it was more my fear of medicine that made me decide to go the natural route. The next couple of hours were pretty tough. My husband and I walked the halls to help speed up the process. When the obstetrician came to check on me I asked how far along I was. When I got to the hospital I was already three centimeters dilated, surely I was much further along now. She asked me what number would make me happy, I said seven or eight centimeters would be nice. She said I was seven and I was satisfied. The truth was that after five hours of walking the hallways I had barely dilated another centimeter. Fortunately, I did not notice her looking at my husband shaking her head. "We are going to speed things up a bit and give you some oxytocin," she said. I knew this would make the contractions much tougher but I wanted to get it over with, so I agreed. The next hour was extremely intense. All I remember were the blue eyes of my husband staring at me with encouragement and amazement, and Shay putting her hands on my back while I was moaning and rocking back and forth trying to catch the contractions. Right when I thought I could not handle another contraction the pain shifted and I got a tremendous urge to push. We called for the obstetrician who checked and told me I was fully dilated. I remember looking at the clock. It was 2:30 pm and I was determined to get this baby out by 3 pm. I pushed and pushed and grunted my way through the next 25 minutes. Naomi's head came into the world at 2:55 pm. The midwife asked me if I wanted to catch her. I did not understand what she meant, but she guided my hands between my legs and I could feel her little shoulders and with my last push I caught her and put her on my chest. My husband was right there to see the miracle of life and was in complete awe. He was also very proud to say that he was the first person she saw, because while her body was still inside me, she opened her eyes and looked right at him.

The nurses came in and wanted to take Naomi to wash her and warm her but I would have none of it. My son had been born in a military hospital. As soon as he was born they took him and I never got to see or hold him until four hours later. There was no way I was going to allow them to take Naomi.

Naomi Nicole was beautiful, pure and perfect when she came into the world. I was completely overwhelmed with an incredible deep Love for this little soul who I knew would be my responsibility for the next 18 years. There is a big difference between the young woman I was with Michael, just excited about becoming a mother without fully realizing what that truly meant, and the woman I had grown into. I was now conscious of the way my childhood had shaped me and how I had shaped my son's life. I knew I wanted something much better for Naomi. Nanny 911 had taught me that consistency was the most important thing about raising a young child. Michael had taught me that a child would rather have negative attention than no attention, and I knew from my own experience that positive feedback got me to do a lot more than negative feedback. Those three principles became the groundwork of the way I chose to parent Naomi.

Today she is 10 years old and I can honestly tell you that it has worked really well for both of us. I have never had a bad day with her, honestly. Do we bicker here or there? Sure.... I guess...not really. My friends think I am a softy, but I don't think so. I am very consistent, but I pick my battles. How much she eats is not as important to me as how kind she is to others. Respect is not something children "should" just give their parents. I believe *true* respect must be earned, and children deserve it as much as adults do. Naomi and I have a deep mutual respect for each other. I have never disciplined her, at least I don't call it that. We all make mistakes, and nobody wants to be yelled at when they already feel bad enough for spilling that glass of milk, or whatever it may be. I will admit that I feel a level of patience towards her that I did not know I possessed. I loved the "terrible twos" and the "trying threes." They just did not feel terrible or trying to me. I loved answering all the "why?" questions. I took the time to really understand her. To me she was a little human being right from the start, somebody that had just as much to teach me as I to teach her, and boy, has she! She showed me my judgments to the world in her childlike acceptance of others. Where I saw a mean remark, she saw somebody who just had a bad day. Where I thought a child was being unkind to her, she saw a person who did not mean to be. Yes, my daughter taught me a lot.

When we were in Tempe, Arizona while I was going to school she was patient with me. She sat with me on the bed for hours on end, playing games on her computer and giving me kisses. I would do things with her as much as my body allowed, which wasn't a lot. We watched a lot of movies together and read a lot of books. She never whined or complained about that time, though I know it wasn't easy on her. Remember in chapter three, when she told me she did not want to see her Dad and I get divorced? In those days, she never let on how sad she felt to be away from him.

It was this deep Love and protection I felt for her that allowed me to hang on during the most difficult and dark days when I would have rather given up. I knew that she would never be the same if I died while she was still a child. She needed me as much as I needed her. Not only did I want to survive this disease, I wanted to thrive. I did not want her to see me suffer, even though there was no way around it. But no matter what, no matter how much I threw up or how much pain I was in, whenever she would walk into the room I would give her a hug and a smile and my world would be okay.

I cannot even begin to pretend to know what it must feel like for a seven-year-old to see her mother in the situation in which she saw me; I can only imagine how terrifying it must have been. We did not have extended family around. No brothers, sister, cousins, uncles, aunts or grandparents for her to go to. No, for her it was just Mommy and Daddy. On top of that, she seemed very aware that we weren't the youngest of parents. This has been a source of stress for her, but I just keep letting her know that we are strong and Mom is beating the MM. Cancer has now been part of nearly a third of her life. She knows Mommy has to go in for treatments once a week, and we text while I am in the hospital. Life goes on as it does in any family, just with a Mommy who has to take breaks for her back but loves to lie on the couch with her and watch TV, read a book together, or chat.

"Getting chemo drugs is like going to a mechanic, giving him lots of money, while he is not obligated to guarantee his services will work"

12

The Joy of Getting Chemo Drugs

*I*magine going to get your car fixed by a mechanic, but before he will do any work you must pay in full, sign all kinds of papers warning you that though he will try to fix your car, many problems may occur as a result of his work, and there is no guarantee that the car will still run. Even better, in some cases it might even crash and be the cause of your death. What I just tried to explain is what pharmaceutical companies have you agree to, pay for, and sign before you can get your prescription.

In the summer of 2015, after being on two different chemo drugs for over a year, the drugs stopped working. One was an oral chemo and the other a weekly infusion. I had to go to the cancer center once a week for treatment. Here my port (a small medical appliance that is installed beneath the skin with a catheter that connects the port to a vein) would be accessed. The nurses had always been happy with my veins but after being poked one too many times they had scarred up and accessing them became harder and more painful. With my port the routine was quite manageable, and the drug was relatively easy to handle; other than some nausea and neuropathy I was doing fairly well. The biggest problem came once a month when I had to get my new oral prescription.

I remember being put on this new drug when I was first diagnosed. My oncologist's nurse found out I was still in childbearing years and went ballistic. She told me that for women in childbearing years getting this drug was a nightmare. Over the course of the next few years I found out what she was talking about. This drug is a derivative of Thalidomide, a sedative drug introduced in the 1950s to treat morning sickness. They soon found that Thalidomide caused serious birth defects. Because of this me, and all women in childbearing years who still have a uterus, have to take a monthly pregnancy test and a medical survey which includes talking to a pharmacist who reminds us monthly that this life saving drug can cause, among many things, a stroke and heart attack, which can severely deform my unborn child if I chose to have another baby with my ribs looking like Swiss cheese and 4 fractured vertebrae! This often turns into a complete disaster. You see, the pregnancy test is only good for one week, and I cannot take this test too soon, because my oncologist can only order the test in the week prior to when I need it. If the two don't line up perfectly, as has often happened, I either need to do another pregnancy test or they need another order from my oncologist. One of the questions is whether I have stopped menstruating for two years. The answer has been yes for over a year now. I was so happy when this finally happened as I thought it was the end of the questionnaire which digs into your private sex life every time. Questions like: Have you had sexual intercourse in the last 4 weeks? NO! Have you used two forms of birth control during the last four weeks? NO, I just abstained from sex for the last couple of years and did not think I needed another form of birth control.

Cancer has taken much from me and my family. One of the things it took was my hormones. In January of 2013, after only two rounds of chemo, my periods suddenly stopped. I had barely turned 45 when from one month to the next, it was gone! Of course I was happy not having to deal with my menses anymore but what I did not realize was how important hormones are when it comes to the strength of our bones and many other physical functions. While Multiple Myeloma had already been attacking my bones, and the steroids were weakening them as well, now, too, my lack of estrogen was causing even more bone loss. Being tall, thin and small boned, all risk factors for osteoporosis, my risk now went through the roof. I was put on a bone builder, a monthly infusion that would help strengthen my bones. Of course when you go to Web MD and research these kinds of drugs, the side effects will make you think twice about using them! I thought it might be interesting for the reader to see what a particular drug used for Multiple Myeloma looks like. Keep in mind this is not even a chemo drug. Things like bone pain, trouble sleeping, and decrease in healthy blood cells were just some of the side effects I had to deal with. Interestingly, some of these side effects are the exact thing that the medicine is supposed to prevent. How can a bone builder have as a side effect a broken femur or necrosis of the jawbone? Well, it does, and it has to be your choice (at strong recommendation of your oncologist) to go ahead and take these drugs anyway. Just for fun here are a few more of the side effects associated with this particular drug: " *Bone Pain, Feeling Weak, High Blood Pressure, Low Amount of Magnesium in the Blood, Low Amount of Potassium in the Blood, Trouble Breathing, Backache, Chills, Chronic Trouble Sleeping, Dizzy, Fluid Retention in the Legs, Feet, Arms or Hands, Flu-Like Symptoms, Joint Pain, Low Energy, Muscle Pain, Throwing Up, Urinary Tract Infection, Abnormally Low Blood Pressure, Anemia, Decreased Blood Platelets, Feeling Restless, Indigestion, Loss of Appetite, Numbness and Tingling, Painful, Red or Swollen Mouth, Upper Abdominal Pain, Abnormal Heart Rhythm, Acquired Decrease of All Cells in the Blood, severe allergic reaction caused by drug, Aseptic Necrosis of Jaw Bone, Atrial Fibrillation, blurred Vision, Fracture of Femur Thigh Bone, Giant Hives, Acute Kidney Disease, Seizures, Anxiety, Arthritis, Chest Pain, Muscle Spasm.*" Just reading these side effects can cause anxiety, and so it is that the medicine cabinet gets fuller and fuller.

When my periods stopped I went to see my endo-crinologist. She did a blood test which showed I had none or extremely low estrogen, progesterone and tes-tosterone. I guess that together with having constant pain and cancer explained why I had no more interest in sex. She told me that my daughter had more hor-mones than I. The good thing for me was that it made my life a lot less complicated and innocent. I had the mind of a child again when it came to sex. No desire, no frustration, no worries. Of course this was not a good thing for my marriage so I used a hormone patch for six months. When my doctor checked six months later there was no change, and she wanted to put me on birth control. One of the side effects was stroke, a nasty and inconvenient side effect that I already had with at least one of my chemo drugs and I declined. Sorry husband, sorry bones, but this is where the negative outweighed the positive. I figured I'd rather my husband get a girl-friend than have me end up with a stroke and Naomi and Michael without a mother.

When this particular chemo drug stopped working I was almost glad as this surely meant no more surveys. The oncologist recommended I start taking the next generation of this drug. I was excited when he told me this newer drug had fewer side effects. Unfortunately, this new drug only had a 10 percent chance of working. Seriously, the FDA allows a chemo drug with a 10 percent chance of working for a certain amount of months (they all quit working) on the market with side effects such as: new cancers, kidney failure that will require dialysis, low immune function and neuropathy. However, the FDA does not allow a patient to try cannabis which helps neuropathy, has never caused a death, is increasingly proven to help with the side effects and, in some instances, may even rid the body of cancer altogether. My oncologist suggested I take the drug with a steroid as that would increase its effectiveness from 10 percent to 30 percent. Again, I felt I had little choice as a new tumor had started to grow on my ribs and was destroying the bone underneath it. Even though steroids had made me nuts before, I chose to have another go at it.

The radiation, chemo and two stem cell transplants had not been able to bring me into complete remission. Now, with the discovery of a new tumor that was again destroying my bones, just two and a half years into my cancer journey, indicating that the Multiple Myeloma

I had was both aggressive and refractory (not respond-ing well to the drugs), I started to seriously look into alternatives to chemo. This brought me to cannabis. I was now almost three years into a possible five-year sur-vival rate. This number was simply not acceptable to me. Not only was my work far from done because I wanted to raise my daughter to become the beautiful woman I knew she would be, but I had become an inspiration to many in the way I handled my diagnosis. I felt a purpose that went way beyond just me and my little family. I was more determined than ever to keep this fight going and cannabis was becoming part of that fight. This meant I was about to become an activist.

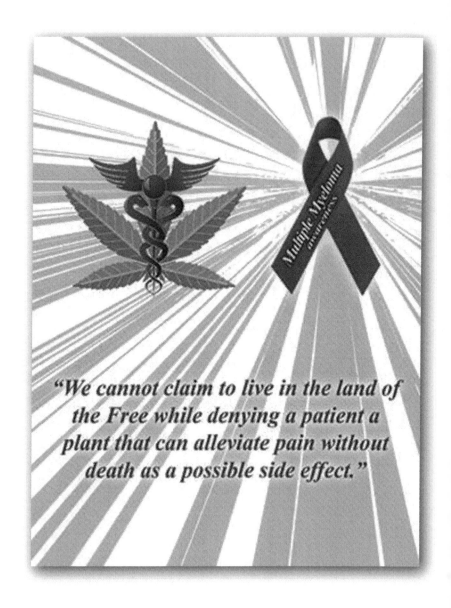

"We cannot claim to live in the land of the Free while denying a patient a plant that can alleviate pain without death as a possible side effect."

13

Gonna Give Cannabis a Try, My Trip to Colorado

*I*n May of 2015 I started actively researching the web for cannabis stories. I knew it was illegal in my state and decided that if I was going to do it, I was going to do it right. At first I started reaching out to politicians, the governor of Texas, a local senator and representatives. I started a Facebook page about my cannabis journey, which I called A Trial of One. I had heard of a trial in Israel where the preliminaries showed a hopeful 60 percent success in the case of Multiple Myeloma. I could not understand how it was possible that a drug could be FDA approved with a 10 percent success rate, yet cannabis, with a possible 60 percent success rate was considered a schedule one drug with jail time attached to it. I also contacted our local newspaper, hoping my story would interest them. I was a woman on a mission. The main issue I wanted to let the world know is that I would have to leave my family in order to see if I could find hope in cannabis. As a European woman that came to the United States of America, the land of the free, I simply could not wrap my head around the fact that cannabis, or marijuana, was considered such an evil drug. Studies from all over the world showed that this was simply not the case. It had been a witch hunt that had started in the 1930's when Spanish immigrants brought marijuana into our country. Up to that point, America actually used cannabis in medicine and Hemp was grown all over the nation, even by our founding fathers and U.S. presidents (e.g. Thomas Jefferson, George Washington, and John Adams). Just as the alcohol prohibition had been a disaster, so was the cannabis prohibition in my eyes. Alcohol really does not do much good to anybody; at least cannabis helps children with epilepsy, eases the pain and nausea for cancer patients and aids other people with debilitating diseases. Coming from Europe I had seen many a bar brawl, but I had never seen that in a marijuana bar. People would sit in a low-lit restaurant; alcohol was not served. There was a menu with different types of hashes or marijuana and people would share their joint while seriously chilling out. The worst thing that could happen to you was gain a few pounds because of getting the "munchies". Anyhow, my purpose was not to get cannabis legalized all the way; I knew that would be a long time coming for Texas. At least I felt people dealing with cancer deserved a chance to give cannabis a try.

Right when I started to look into this, the Texas House came together to vote on a Bill brought forward by a very conservative Republican. He said that as this was God's plant, we should all have the right to use it. I was writing e-mails and making phone calls left and right. Only one representative actually took the time to call me. This was due to his secretary who was in tears when she heard my story, and my plan to leave the state in hopes of finding a cure or at least natural relief from the side effects of the cancer and chemo. Many of the secretaries showed a lot of sympathy, but I could tell that I was in a losing battle. About a week into my search, the Bill was denied by the Governor. I was deeply disappointed, but more determined than ever as I felt the tumor growing.

I found my first place on Craigslist (yes, the reader is wise to see a red flag with that statement). Though cannabis is legal in Colorado, there are plenty of places that don't favor it. I found this out as I was looking for both a room to stay and an oncologist to see. I always like to be honest and up front. In doing so I hope others treat me likewise. When I called a Multiple Myeloma specialist in Colorado, I explained to the assistant why I was coming to Colorado and what my plans were. I told her I wished to continue using chemotherapy, while at the same time I would start using cannabis in hopes of not needing all my other medicines. I figured if cannabis did what they said it could, I would be able to get off my pain medication, neuropathy meds, anti-depressants and anxiety drugs, and my anti-nausea medication, a total of five medicines I would not have to use anymore, something my body would surely thank me for. Prior to my mentioning cannabis she was bubbly and polite. As soon as I said cannabis she became quiet and distant and told me she needed to ask the doctor. Her response was, of course, an indicator as to how the oncologist felt about cannabis and, lo and behold, I received a call at the end of the day stating that the doctor did not approve of the use of cannabis and wouldn't see me. I tried to remind the assistant that it might get me off the other opioids and drugs I was on which were causing a lot of strain on my system; she said little in return and we hung up. I realized that finding acceptance of cannabis would prove more difficult than I thought, even in Colorado. Fortunately, I ended up with a Multiple Myeloma specialist who was okay with the use of cannabis and, though he did not personally promote it (doctors can't without the proper trials and research), he was glad I let him know about my plan and was fine with my using it.

Next I needed to look for a place to stay. A friend had suggested I start a GoFundMe page which had brought in what seemed to be enough money for rent, transportation and medicine, but by no means would it allow me my own apartment so I had to look for a roommate. Most places on Craigslist were too expensive. I was looking for about $500 a month and many were asking between $750 and $1,250 per month. I wanted and needed to take my service dog Coco with me. Otherwise she would have to be by herself all day with me gone, my husband working and my daughter at school. Plus, she was my dog, not my family's and, therefore, my responsibility.

I love my dog, Coco. She is a nine-pound chiweenie (Chihuahua/dachshund) and a super sweet snuggle dog. Her sole purpose in life seems to be to lie with me and be petted by me. She is not interested in playing or chewing and acts like a very old dog until she sees another dog, child or squirrel. Then she acts like a hyperactive two-year-old pup chasing the child or squirrel down the street. My neighbors must have had a hard time believing what a sweetheart she really is, because she only shows her noisy, obnoxious side in our neighborhood. The way I got her deserves to be told before I go on with my story because, in a way, we saved each other.

I had gone to our local pet store on a Saturday a year earlier to get our dog, Gizmo, some food. As with many Saturdays, the local ASPCA had several dogs visiting the pet store in hopes of finding them a home. As soon as I walked in, I saw this tiny, little black dog, very thin and nervous. Though I am a bit intimidated by little dogs, as you never know if they will come at you and bite, I felt a strong urge to hold her. I asked the volunteer if it was okay to pick her up. She said yes and I took this little girl in my arms. She was shaking, very thin and smelly with patches of her hair missing and her ears completely bald. My heart went out to her and, since my daughter and I volunteered at the ASPCA, I asked if I could take her home and give her a bath. Of course she said yes. On weekends the dogs are mostly left in their cages by themselves, and it is always appreciated when somebody wants to take one home for the weekend. Because we already had a puppy, I also wanted to see how they got along. Before we got Gizmo, I had talked to my daughter about getting an older, more laid back, lap dog. As a young girl she, of course, wanted a "play" dog. Even though I knew having a puppy would be a lot of work, my daughter got her wish when we found Gizmo who was in desperate need of a home. We both loved him very much, but it soon became clear that I was the main caretaker of Gizmo. I was still open to finding an older dog who would hopefully chill Gizmo out and become his playmate, and perhaps meet my need for a "lap dog."

After I took Coco home and bathed her, she was on my lap for the rest of the day. I had pretty much fallen in love with her. By Monday it seemed she was not doing so well. She was having digestive issues and was passing the smelliest gas I have ever smelled coming from such a little dog. I gave her yoghurt and added some coconut oil to her food. I made an appointment with the vet and we went to see her that day. The vet told me she thought Coco was about 4 years old (though I thought she was older as she had quite a bit of grey on her snout). She had a rash on her belly, weighed in at seven pounds, which was way too thin, but otherwise seemed okay. Seventy-eight dollars later with a prescription for antibiotics, I left the vet and considered taking Coco back to the ASPCA. This dog was going to cost me money and energy, neither of which I had a lot off. I did not think it smart to take on a "trouble" dog. Not knowing her history, where she had gotten the nips in her ear and how her demeanor might be once she was better, adopting her seemed like something I should not take on at that point in my life. She sat on my lap and our eyes met. It was in that moment that I realized she had issues, possibly big issues, just like me, and it was with that thought that I knew I could never let her go. What if my husband and daughter decided that, though I was a sweet and nice Mom and wife, they did not really want me anymore because I could become too expensive and had too many issues? That is the problem with being an empathetic person, you tend to put yourself in the shoes of others all the time, whether it is wise to do so or not.

I do believe that we empaths make this world a sweeter place. We do our best to follow the golden rule. We try our hardest to do unto others as we would have others do unto us. My empathy has always extended beyond the human race and into the animal kingdom, to the point that I capture the bugs in our house and take them outside because I don't feel I have the right to "murder" them. Silly, I know, but that is me. The only animal I don't extend this courtesy to is the mosquito, because as Sylvester Stallone says in Rambo: "They drew blood first!"

Unfortunately, Gizmo passed before he was a year old. My daughter had a really hard time with his death. One day he was fine, the next he was pooping and throwing up blood and I had to take him to the emergency room only to have the doctor tell me 6 hours and $900 later that he had passed away. The cause was never found. Naomi read months later that dogs can die from eating grapes and felt guilty because she had given him a grape. I think I have been able to convince her that this was not the cause, that there may have been something in the backyard that he had gotten a hold of which caused him to be poisoned. Watching her grief for Gizmo made me more determined than ever to beat this cancer that had invaded my body. I could not bear to think how she would react if I died before she was a grown woman. I simply did not see that as an option, and so I would do anything it took to stay healthy!

Most people I contacted did not allow pets and if they did, they did not allow the use of cannabis. I did not know how I was going to take the cannabis and I knew that smoking it might be one option, so there was no sense in hiding my intentions. Unlike what I and probably many people think, Colorado has not become a state where everybody hangs out and gets stoned. Colorado seems to be as conservative as it is liberal, and there are plenty of people not happy with the legalization of cannabis. I finally came across an ad that spoke about wanting a "spiritual" housemate who was open to "alternative" health practices. I figured this person was talking about cannabis and gave her a call.

Bobby seemed like a really nice and knowledgeable woman. Soft spoken and sincere, she came across as somebody who cared deeply about the welfare of others. She told me she had "cured" two other housemates of cancer: one with colon cancer and one with kidney cancer. She gave me the number of one lady, who I contacted. Although this woman did not have late stage cancer, she nonetheless was free of cancer after a surgery and using the recommended Rick Simpson Oil, a high THC cannabis oil that was first used by Rick Simpson in

Canada, and which has gotten the unofficial reputation of curing many cancers. The protocol is pretty intense. A patient has to use a gram of oil per day over a 60-day period. It was said that many would see their tumors shrink and their cancer disappear. I had tried so many natural remedies following my knowledge and passion, none of which had helped much. Garlic had seemed to keep my white blood cells higher, but as far as vitamin C, vitamin D, greens, mushrooms, C0-enzyme Q10 and many other promised herbs and supplements, I had seen no improvement. As a self-described cannabis "virgin" I was quite nervous about using this much THC. Though I was born and raised in Europe, in a very progressive, tolerant and open minded country, I had never felt the need to try marijuana. Unlike what some people and politicians think, the legalization of cannabis does not result in more abuse of the drug. Ask anybody who is not interested in cigarettes or alcohol. Just because we can get it, doesn't mean we want to use it. Another argument in favor of legalizing cannabis: those who wish to get stoned are already doing so, regardless of what the law says. It is amazing how many people I have met that have offered me marijuana here in Texas. Sometimes it seems I am the only one who isn't using it.

While in college in North Dakota I had given in to peer pressure on two occasions and smoked a bit of marijuana.

Both times left me feeling anxious and paranoid and had left me uninterested in the drug. Now, more than 20 years later, I was hoping that taking cannabis might be the way to complete remission or at least lead to a life with fewer pain medications and pharmaceutical drugs. I expressed my concerns to Bobby and she guaranteed me that it was her job to make sure I would dose properly and she would be there for me all the way. She did tell me that my stay with her would be no vacation. Her house-mates were expected to help out with cooking and cleaning. Not being the kind of person who likes to sit around all day, I agreed with her and said I welcomed the idea of being useful. She also told me that she had some bad luck with roommates in the past and that she would need to do a back ground check on me to make sure I was okay. I had no issues with that as I knew she would find nothing other than maybe a speeding ticket.

Bobby lived in Oswald, Colorado, a small and conservative town about 35 minutes north of Denver. I looked on the map while at home and it appeared to be fairly close to Denver. When I arrived she was there to pick me up. We hugged and I felt good about her and the whole deal. We went out to dinner where she immediately gave me half a grain of the Rick Simpson Oil to see how I would react. I was tired, excited and a bit nervous and we talked for a long time. It is interesting how people on the spiritual path seem to think they can point out and solve our life's problems in a one-hour conversation. She seemed to have figured me and my issues out pretty much right away (adding issues where there were none). Even though I felt some red flags during our first conversation, I decided to run with the situation and see how it would pan out.

By the time she dropped me off at my hotel I was extremely tired. She continued to look at me closely and kept asking me how I felt. If I was high, I did not notice it because I was dealing with so many feelings and emotions. She left me and I went to bed and had a decent night sleep. The next day she took me to her house which seemed less than optimal. On our drive, she told me that she kept a very clean house, but when she opened the door, the first thing that welcomed me was the distinct smell of a home that has three dogs and 12 cats living in it. The house was very dusty and looked unfinished, something she blamed on what previous tenants had done. She said they had practically gutted the house while she was in Arizona and taken thousands of dollars of stuff.

Bobby was a tiny woman with a very serious disposition. Not even a hundred pounds with a back brace due to an accident she looked like a victim to me and my heart went out to her. Over the next couple of weeks, she was eager to tell me how many people had done her wrong, something that turned out to be very much self-imposed, but let me not get ahead of my story. The room for rent currently had a couple in it who had also misled her in their promises and seemed to be just hanging out getting stoned all day. The room was in the basement, had no windows or a door that could close, and was behind a fake closet. Before the reader starts to wonder why in the hell I did not run out the house right away, please put yourself in my shoes. First off, I do have a high tolerance, and even acceptance, for the unusual. I have lived in much worse conditions and I did not know at that moment where else to go. Being easy going and willing to put up with a lot, and desperate to see if cannabis could help me, I felt being in a house with somebody with knowledge about cannabis who was willing to monitor me was the best opportunity I was going to get. I knew I did not want to be in a place by myself experimenting with the THC and the unfortunate side effect of getting high and paranoid, so I decided to let my adventurous side lead me and I gave her the required $500 deposit for the room, figuring I would clean the house and make it more livable.

That morning she gave me my next dose. Later I found out that, especially with small women such as myself, one should stick with the low dose of half a grain for about seven days before upping it. She, however, wanted me to go to the size of a grain of rice. Since I thought I had felt nothing the night before I agreed. I figured the years of using heavy pain medication had made me more tolerant and I was hoping this would be easier than I expected. She squeezed the oil, which is a tar like substance, out of a syringe and gave it to me. It seemed more than a grain of rice to me, but she said it was just like a long grain of rice. The taste of Cannabis is hard to describe for those who have never tried it. It is very earthy and pungent; not horrible, but not enjoyable either. It was very sticky and it stuck to my teeth, making them black. One day too much got on my hand and I tried to wash it off. It is so oily and thick that it is extremely hard to get off. I felt fine half an hour later and we decided to go out and have lunch, my treat. As she had been emphasizing how she had been used so much in her life I wanted to be that person to show her there were still good people in the world, so I made it a point to help out a lot, pay for most things and be a person that she could trust.

When we were almost done with lunch I started to feel a bit weird. The first thing I noticed was my time perception. We were talking and all of a sudden it occurred to me that we had been in that restaurant for quite a while. I told her about how I felt and she said she could tell by the way I looked that I was getting high. I excused myself and went to the bathroom. When I got out of the stall it felt like I must have been in the bathroom forever and I figured she was probably worried about what I was doing. When I got back to the table I told her this, and she said I was barely gone. As we left the restaurant I felt a bit shaky, but I figured this was all part of the deal and I was going along with it, knowing I had a seasoned caregiver with me. She took me to the library where I sat in a chair while she did stuff with the computer. A couple of times she would get up to do something else (I have no clue what since I was trying very hard to keep my composure by that time). When she got back she would ask me how I felt and although I was feeling extremely strange and a bit paranoid (surely the people around me must have seen how messed up I was) I told her I was okay. I did get a bit annoyed because she would leave me for an hour at a time, or so I thought. She later told me she was not gone longer than a couple of minutes, but my time perception was completely distorted. I finally told her we needed to go and as I got up I noticed I had a hard time standing and walking straight. I felt like a drunk with a severe case of paranoia. This was no fun at all! We drove home and I told her I really did not feel good and just needed to lie down. Back at her place she took me to the basement where her bedroom was as well which she shared with 5 kittens she was treating for ringworm! I climbed straight into bed, told her I was thirsty and nauseous and after what seemed like hours she came back with a bucket and some coke which apparently could help with the high. As I laid there in paralysis and paranoia, I realized how I really did not know this woman at all and now I was at her complete mercy. All kinds of scary thoughts crossed my mind, anywhere from her coming in and killing me to my not being able to swallow and choking on my own tongue. Thankfully most of the thoughts I forgot as soon as they came in. I was able to doze off a bit while the kitties were climbing all over me, and she came in to check on me a couple of times. This whole episode took a total of about four hours, but to me it was like living in a nightmare for much longer. When I finally started to feel like myself again, I got up and went upstairs. I told her everything and she did admit she likely gave me a bit too much too soon. Unfortunately, this was not a good way to start with the treatment and in the end it proved to be the reason why I was never able to build up my tolerance beyond a grain and a half.

I stayed in Colorado for a couple of days and applied for my medical cannabis card. I had told Bobby that I found a place in Denver that sold the Rick Simpson Oil (RSO) at a very reasonable rate. Purchasing a month supply of RSO came out to about $17 per day. She told me she made her own, and wanted me to try that first. Since I had no opportunity to go to the dispensary I agreed to use her oil until I found out how she made it. As I continued to pay for our lunches and dinners when we were out, she charged me $100 for going with me to get my Cannabis card. She also told me I needed to ask for the right to own 25 plants as I was a super special person (her way of saying I was a late stage cancer patient). I did not understand this as I figured I would be long gone before the plants would even mature, but since she said she would teach me how to make the oil and I was using her oil now, I agreed. This meant spending $200 more on getting the license, but I figured it was all for a good cause, so I agreed.

I left a couple of days later and the following week my daughter and husband accompanied me on the drive so I would have a car for the next two months. Needless to say, when they saw the house they were less than impressed, even though Naomi fell in love with the dogs and kitties. They stayed with me for a week at a hotel while I tried to make my room and the downstairs more like home. It was hard to do with the boxes and mess all around, but beggars can't be choosers. I gave Bobby another $500 and more money for the oil I had already used. After a week Richard and Naomi had to go home, and I started to seriously dose the RSO. Up to that point

I only did it in the evening because I did not want to be high around my daughter. It helped me sleep, and I had noticed that my neuropathy (a side effect from the chemo) was gone! Even though this was very hopeful, I was disappointed that the nausea that had plagued me for three years wasn't going away, but actually had gotten worse. Later I realized it was not so much the cannabis, but rather the situation I was in that left me anxious and depressed.

The house had three more roommates. A nice couple who was there temporarily. The guy was a veteran and suffered from PTSD. He seemed to be helped by the oil, was super nice and a true gentleman, helping out where he could. His girlfriend was a sweetheart and I enjoyed their company. There was another lady who pretty much stayed in her room at all times. I do not know what her issue or role was in the house, other than she swore all the time yet claimed to be an elder who had figured out all of life's issues and thought the rest of us were idiots. To me she made little sense and sounded like an angry, obnoxious old woman, but to each their own.

It had become clear to me during this time that Bobby thought I was a victim of my cancer and circumstances and she treated me like an injured child. She kept pushing me to take more of the oil and even started putting them in capsules at higher doses than I was comfortable with. Instead of taking her capsules I would take the oil straight from the syringe making sure the amount was within my comfort zone. After a week of using the oil two or three times a day (depending how bad the high would get) I started looking at different ways of taking it. Coco was an absolute life-saver during these moments, as she would lie with me in bed while I would stare at her desperately waiting for the paranoia to wear off. Someone had told me I could take the oil as a suppository without the psychoactive affects and I tried doing so. This turned out to be a very messy and literal pain in the butt, so I gave that up when somebody else suggested I put it in my vagina (oh the things we try to stay ahead of cancer). This, too, turned out to be a big mess as it seemed to all come back out. I never got high doing it this way, probably because it never got absorbed. I did, however, get sore and had to go back to taking it orally. Bobby kept on me about taking more than I wanted to. She became the cannabis police and I started to realize that she had not much else to talk about than cannabis. When we were out and about it was all about visiting different dispensaries and being in the car with her became a chore because it seemed she was very angry at the world. There weren't many people that did not get verbally attacked by Bobby, and I started to seriously doubt her level of spirituality.

I went home for a week because I did not want to miss out on my daughter's and husband's birthdays, and Naomi had a piano recital I wanted to attend. Yes, keeping cannabis illegal in some states really does tear families apart. It was great being home with my family and I did not want to go back to Colorado where my home was a basement room without windows, a very unhappy caretaker and too many animals, but I felt I needed to stick this one out. The paper had done a front page story on me and people had given me money. This wasn't just about me anymore, and I needed to find out for everybody whether this would help me or not.

So I went back to Colorado. Bobbie was very much against eating any kind of bird; when I asked her why she said the story was too horrible to tell so we left it at that. She owned some beautiful birds and I figured she simply was too much of a bird lover to eat chicken or turkey. When I came back and was in my bedroom trying to get through another Rick Simpson THC high, she came in and showed me a video on her computer. She told me to watch it but that she had to leave because it was too horrifying to her. I had no clue what this was all about but I watched the video. It showed some of her birds had been brutally attacked and mutilated. Their heads and wings had been ripped off and it was a horrible scene. Who would do such a thing? She came back into my room, sat on my bed and started to tell me what had happened with tears in her eyes. I felt horrible for her and the birds, yet did not understand why she would have such insensitivity to share such a horrible story right in the midst of my THC paranoia high. She then told me how she had another roommate who had killed herself in the upstairs bedroom. I became scared. This house, which was supposed to be a spiritual house of healing, had turned into a house of horror where people got stoned, birds were murdered, cats and dogs had ringworm, and someone had committed suicide. I have always been the emotional caretaker of people but when I came to Colorado to try cannabis, I paid money and needed to be taken care of. Yet once again, I found myself being at the listening end of somebody else's problems and I no longer felt safe in that house.

That afternoon she took me out into the shed and showed me how she made the RSO. The shed was dirty and dusty. We had to pour many bottles of alcohol in with the leaves and flowers that I had ground up the previous day and the fumes were quite strong. It was hot and stifling in the shed, and after watching her take the cannabis from one bucket into another with unsanitary hands that had not been washed and buckets that did not seem too clean either, I had seen enough and left.

The next day I went to the dispensary and bought a month's supply of Rick Simpson Oil. Almost immediately Bobby's attitude toward me changed. I had told the lady at the counter how I had reacted to the cannabis and how it was made. She frowned and said I should only buy legitimate and properly tested oil, and that many people tried to push extra oil on their clients in order to make more money. I stayed in the house for another week at which time Bobby no longer spoke to me. She no longer looked in on me when I was high and whatever negative energy she said people brought to the house, I could now clearly see was actually coming from her.

I wrote her a letter asking for my deposit back. It was about 12 days before November, but there was no way I could stay in this house and I desperately wanted to leave. The letter was kind yet to the point. I told her that the house was not healthy for me, that the stories had frightened me, and that I did not feel comfortable using her oil. Even though she wanted me to keep track of the hours I worked, I told her not to worry about the money she might owe me for that. I told her I would continue working (I had been painting, dusting, mopping etc.) so that she would not feel used. I told her it was nothing personal, but I needed to be in an emotionally healthy place to heal and I simply did not feel comfortable at her house anymore.

Days later I received a letter saying that I had signed a lease which stated I had to give a month notice and I was not going to get the money back. So much for her insisting it wasn't about the money. I had only stayed at her house for two weeks, during which I had paid for groceries, dinners, and done a lot of fixing up. I had made sure to stay busy and show her I cared about her and the house, and here was the thanks I got. After leaving her place I refused to lose trust in people. I had made it this far in life without turning into the bitter woman she was even though I had just as much reason to become that. I realized the issue was hers and had nothing to do with me. Sure, losing the money did not feel good, but at least I knew I would be out of this place of negativity. Bobby will be in that place until she wakes up and realizes it is not her roommates that are the issue, but it is her that needs healing. This was a typical case of "you can't change what you don't acknowledge!"

Interestingly, about a month later her roommate (the elder lady) who was very much Bobbie's guide and friend, emailed me to inform me that she too had been kicked out and had been branded a fake and a fraud. She asked me if she could stay at the place I had found in Boulder, Colorado. Through a newfound friend I had found a wonderful and loving place that I was to call home for my second month in Colorado. The couple who owned the house was amazing and I am happy to say we have become dear friends. There was no way I was going to introduce these kind people to the energy I had endured in Oswald and I chose not to answer the letter.

"Though my life has been far from easy, it most certainly has been very good."

14

Climbing to the Top of the Mountain

*A*t the beginning of my cannabis research I had been put in touch with Neshama, a very kind, soft spoken yet passionate lady. She was the Communications Director of the National Hemp Association, and she had a tremendous amount of knowledge about the world of Industrial Hemp. Together with her husband, Zev, they worked tirelessly to make the growth and production of Hemp legal in all 50 states.

Hemp is in the cannabis family, but is grown for all kinds of uses, such as highly nutritious food as Hemp "hearts" or seeds, hemp oil, clothing, shoes, textiles, animal bedding, paper, auto parts, biofuel etc. Though we lost touch over the summer, we reconnected when things were getting out of hand at Bobbie's place. Neshama asked if I wanted to meet her at the University of Colorado at Boulder, where her daughter was going to do a video interview with a researcher who was working on a cannabis project. I happily agreed. After the interview we went out for lunch and I talked about my living arrangement. She told me she had a friend I might be able to stay with. We met Cedar, who owned a beautiful home right across the street from an amazing park that accessed the foothills of the Rocky Mountains. The house had a homey feel to it, with a happy yellow front door, signs and decorations that showed the people in the house cared deeply about our planet and all its inhabitants, promoting a loving, healthy and peaceful existence. She agreed to take me in for the month of November. Cedar could tell I really did not want to spend one more night in the basement in Oswald, and told me I could go ahead and spend the last couple of days in October at her place before I would go back to Texas for a week to celebrate Halloween. I cried with relief and when she gave me a big hug, I knew everything would be alright.

The interesting thing I learned through my traveling back and forth was how effective the THC was in treating my pain and neuropathy. I never once reached for my pain medication while in Colorado using the THC. I might have thought this was due to the change in treatment if it wasn't for the fact that I would have to go back on my meds every time I went back to Texas. I continued to stay in touch with our local newspaper, representatives, governor and senator about the positive effect cannabis was having on me. I was very open in my conversations about cannabis back at home and on Facebook. I understand that even today many people are still strongly opposed to cannabis and I believe this is due to a lack of education and a purposeful misguidance by the government.

I have told my daughter that I don't like drugs, cigarettes, alcohol, donuts, and soda, amongst many things. I also tell her I am okay with moderation and I believe that we have the right to choose how we wish to live our lives with all the consequences that come with it. When she was about four years old and uninterested in brushing her teeth, I told her I understood and it would be her choice. I also told her that cavities hurt and that if I was her I would make sure to keep my teeth clean so I wouldn't have to worry about cavities. She has always been good about brushing her teeth. When she showed interest in eating too much candy and was curious about soft drinks, I told her it was okay to drink and eat but I also told her that too much sugar could cause tooth decay, obesity and diabetes later down the road. She decided sodas weren't worth it and she hardly eats candy. I never lectured her, I never said no, I simply explained the consequences of these kinds of habits. We have talked the same way about cigarettes, alcohol and drugs. I have told her it is not a smart idea to start any of these as it is very hard to overcome an addiction, so why put yourself in that situation. She is for cannabis but only because she has seen how it helped me; however, she is not interested in trying it because I have told her that the high is very uncomfortable and made me paranoid. I don't know if I have a special child who is easily persuaded by what I tell her, and I don't know if this will change as she gets older. I do know I believe in picking my battles. I am more concerned with her being a decent and caring human being than wearing the "appropriate" clothes while being a sneaky child because she has a mother who says no to everything. One thing I have told her is that lying is unacceptable to me because its consequence is that we can never truly trust each other again. I know it has made a deep impact on her because she is very open to me about everything! I also know she feels comfortable doing so because I have never judged her for her thoughts and ideas. We discuss things openly and honestly. We look at things from different directions and usually she, herself, will come up with the right thing to do.

Cannabis should never be used by somebody whose brain is still developing unless it is needed to treat a disorder that is benefitted by its use. However, I see no difference between having a glass of wine after work as compared to the joint my friend has in the evening with her husband. Call me ignorant, but I do not believe cannabis is any more a gateway drug than alcohol is. I have tried a lot of things in my life, and even though my life was tough enough that I could have slipped down that hole, I never got addicted to anything.

It is also my understanding that in many cases it is the lifestyle that causes the addiction not the addiction that causes the lifestyle, though I have nothing but my instinct and common sense behind this belief. Yes, I am sure there are people in this world that have a perfect life, choose to experiment with drugs and become horribly addicted, losing everything in the process. What I think more often happens, though, is a person does not have such a great life, either physically or emotionally, and therefore reaches for something to ease their pain. If this happens I believe that things can turn around when the situation gets better. It is in the same way that so many college students experiment with drugs. Yet most graduates do not go on binge drinking or smoking pot. For me, this is a fight for the right to use cannabis in my battle with cancer, and I want the right to use what I deem to be most effective and least damaging for my body. You see, Multiple Myeloma is not the kind of cancer you get, treat and either die from or get better from. Multiple Myeloma is a cancer you need to learn to live with. Quality of life becomes a big issue after years of treatment. I always told my oncologist that quality is even more important to me than quantity. I do not want to wither away in front of my family's eyes. I want to live for as long and as healthy as I can and when that is no longer possible, I am ready to move on. Because cannabis was great at treating numerous side effects, without the toxicity to my body, I will continue to fight for my right (and the right of others) to use it. What is interesting to see is that the country seems ready to legalize medicinal cannabis with more than 50 percent of Americans in favor of legalization. Unfortunately, many people have to choose between leaving their jobs and friends behind or using cannabis, a natural plant that is much less toxic on the system than the oxycodone, OxyContin, morphine and many other very addicting drugs a Multiple Myeloma patient can very easily get. We need these drugs to be able to handle the destruction that our bodies have endured, but I feel that we should have a choice in the matter as to which "poison" we want to use.

Early November I arrived back in Colorado. It was nice how smooth my flights had been, considering it was just me and Coco, neither one of us particularly strong. This time the flight had been a bit challenging. We had a toddler on the plane. Before boarding I had seen her, this adorable little girl, about three years old. She was just a tiny little thing and looked like a little doll. As we went on board the plane, she had smiled at me and Coco.

It is amazing how much noise can come from such a little girl. Although she was about four rows in front of me, her screeching and hollering went right through me. She was angry that she had to sit still and she was determined to let us all know she was not happy during the ENTIRE FLIGHT!!!! I chose to take her screaming as an opportunity to meditate my way through the flight which kept me in my "happy place." Other than the little girl the flight was uneventful. Coco was amazing as always and I felt an immense gratitude for not having to take on this journey by myself. I had survived my disastrous stay at Bobbie's house, I had survived a difficult childhood, I had survived three years of chemo, stem cell transplants and radiation, and I had come out of it stronger, happier and more grateful than ever. Life had become sweeter somehow. I knew my time was limited and that was okay. I was living life with the strongest intent of making every moment count. Somewhere along the line a deep inner peace had come over me. I had surrendered to what was happening and, though this in no way meant I had given up, it did mean that I was going to do all I could to make my life and the lives of those around me as good as possible, and other than that let it all go. The only worry left was not being with my daughter. It made me a better mother though, because I wanted to make sure I would teach her all I knew about this amazing place called Earth. This place that I believed we choose to come to grow and learn and Love and live the best that we can!

Traveling with a little dog, a backpack and a computer, while bones and body are frail is quite the ordeal, especially going through security. It took me quite a while to get the harness on which carried Coco. After that I had to put on my back pack and get Coco to lay in her little doggy bag, something that took quite a bit of coaxing. My husband helped me as we said our goodbyes (Naomi chose to stay with friends as the goodbyes were too hard on her) then I walked away blowing my husband one last kiss before going through security. Once there I had to take everything back off! It was inconvenient enough taking shoes, jacket, belt and backpack (computer separately in a tray, please) off when flying. Doing all this while trying to keep a little dog calm with loud noises and strange people all around was quite an undertaking, yet somehow we managed every time. I was allowed to hold her as we went through security. On the other side things got even more complicated as I was trying to get her, my clothes, computer and back pack situated again. Thankfully the world is full of nice people and I would get the help I needed. It is amazing how heavy a nine-pound dog and a computer with some personal items feels, but we managed.

My husband had asked if I could stay in a hotel near the airport when I arrived at 10.30 PM that night. He is my eternal worrier, quite the opposite from myself. Blame it on my frugal nature or my stubborn perseverance, but of course I did not listen to him. I would rather make the journey all the way to my second home, my nice little room in Boulder, about 50 minutes from the airport, than to check in and out of a hotel again. And so it was that I arrived back at my little studio at 11.30 on Saturday night, November 7th. Coco and I made ourselves comfortable. Unpacking could wait till morning. Food, who needs it, just give me Netflix and I was out like a light in less than 10 minutes.

We woke up to 30 degrees F. I do not believe I have felt it that cold since I moved to Texas 10 years earlier when our daughter was three months old. It was 83 the day we left with lows not yet in the fifties. Both Coco and I are wimps when it comes to the cold. I don't like to complain about the heat especially after surviving five winters in Minot, North Dakota. Mosquitoes are an entirely different story and even though it was almost mid-November we still had plenty of mosquitoes to deal with back at home in Texas. So many that it was hard to enjoy a nice walk outside without being continuously attacked by the little buggers. I remember walking Coco during one of our famous mosquito outbreaks. Although it was

90 degrees outside, I was walking in jeans, a scarf, winter boots and a long-sleeved t-shirt, all in order to try and avoid the little beasts. You might ask why not use some bug spray, but with all the chemicals already in my blood, I figured I did not want to add to it, and it seems that Lake Jackson mosquitoes just laugh at the "natural" bug spray. As we were walking, or I should say running, not even giving poor Coco a chance to go potty because the mosquitoes would attack us as soon as we slowed down, I saw one of my neighbors walking her dog, leisurely, in shorts and a t-shirt, not bothered by mosquitoes in the least. I was thinking that the bugs were either only attracted to me, or she had gone through a whole bottle of deet. I would wear the same attire when mowing grass in 90-degree heat. I would wear my yoga pants under my jeans, wear a t-shirt under my husband's long sleeve t-shirt with a scarf, a hat and gloves. This look was finished off with my big boots and thick glasses. This indeed worked to keep the mosquitoes away but it also made me lose about five pounds in water weight every time.

Although words could not express how hard it was for me to leave my daughter during this time in my life, Boulder and my little studio felt like my second home. A place where nature was still at its best, where the food at the local neighborhood store was nothing but organic, where there were more recycling cans than trashcans, and where it seemed like every other house had a solar panel. A place where there were bike trails and plenty of parks, with people actually using them! I felt at home in Boulder; here I felt my soul rejuvenating and my spirit rising. Feeling the fresh mountain air, knowing my red blood cells would multiply to keep up with the altitude, everything seemed just a little better here. Of course, the place was completely unaffordable, and I would have to ship my neighbors, my friends and Naomi's friends here in order to make it just right, but hey, one can dream.

I went to the neighborhood coffee store where I ordered my coffee and a chocolate zucchini bread, interestingly delicious with chocolate chip chunks. I made some small talk with the locals, petted a cute little dog who we would later meet on our climb to the top of the mountain. Back home, Coco met me at the door, how dare I forget her, she had become my partner in crime going with me everywhere I went and she did not like being separated from me anymore. Coco and I went to go shopping next and of course at nine pounds and 100 percent cuteness in her little service dog jacket, she got a lot of attention. There was a time I was the one that made heads turn, but between Coco and Naomi, that time is long gone and I am okay with that.

After lunch with the temperature at 57 degrees I decided it was time for our walk around Wonderland Lake. The lake was one of the reasons I fell in love with this place. I stayed less than a five-minute walk from the most amazing view of what Colorado is all about to me. The foothills of the mountains, fresh air, a beautiful lake and miles and miles of trails going around the lake and up the mountain. The Colorado sun felt hot, even at 57 degrees. Coco, who was not used to these kinds of walks, was dragging behind, needing to sniff every blade of grass and I carried her much of the way. For me, there is nothing like hiking in nature. Being part of nature, is like being part of God, the Universe, and the Whole. It is where we came from, and though I much appreciate the comforts of our modern existence, I realize how much my spirit needs to go outdoors and enjoy beautiful hikes. There were many people on the trails, most of them with dogs. People jogging, women walking together happily chatting, couples holding hands, teenagers giggling. Many people were also riding bikes, both mountain bikes and road bikes. It was a day like I had not had in a very long time and sharing it with all these people made it all the more special.

We got to a turnoff that would either take us around the lake, beautiful and familiar since I had done it several times, or a skinny trail that would wind me ever higher and steeper to the top. I hesitated. I had not brought water, my bones were frail, I had not brought my phone. Even though I heard my husband's voice of concern in the back of my mind, I brushed it off and decided to take on the challenge. With every step I took I felt exhilaration, like I was overcoming something, like I was growing in spirit as I had so many times on this journey we call Life. I felt I had to keep going, to laugh cancer in its face, to show who was boss. I started talking to my body. I was telling her how strong she was, how every step up and forward made my muscles and bones stronger, closing the holes cancer had caused in my bones. I felt my lungs expand, my blood rejuvenate, my heart pump in a way I had forgotten it could from when I was a triathlete. With my inner eye I saw my body find its balance, pushing the Myeloma out of my bone marrow, sweating it out for the wind to carry off. I felt myself getting stronger, not just physically, but mentally, the kind off toughness that comes from not giving up, not letting go, persevering, going against the odds, not taking no for an answer.

There was a nice man ahead of me with a very big back pack, I slowly caught up with him. He was a bit overweight and struggling. I asked if he was using the back pack as extra exercise, he smiled and pointed to the top of the mountain. "No," he said, "I come here to hang glide, it is beautiful coming down, and I use the climb as my exercise. It is hard but it is well worth it." He was clearly out of breath, and so was I. We stood and chatted for a while, then I took off again. After about a 100-yard climb, feeling my heart in my throat I saw a large rock I could sit on and decided to take another break. Coco was clearly not into this climb and I mostly had to carry her. When we got to the rock we sat down and admired the incredible view below. I saw another lake in the distance and some hills around. Although it was November, it was still very green and lush. A man came down the path and I asked him if we were about half way up and he said not quite yet. I started to doubt if this was such a good idea. I began to think that maybe this was not such a wise and healthy decision. At that time the man with the back pack had caught up with me again. I told him about my diagnosis and that I wanted to go to the top of the mountain as a challenge in beating this thing inside of me, but I wasn't sure I could. He told me I should do it for sure then, that I should not let the cancer keep me from doing this amazing trail. Seeing how much he was struggling, I knew I needed to do it as well. Fear started creeping in as it sometimes can when we push the envelope. I had physically overdone it before in my life, not always with the greatest of consequences. One time I had done a six mile run after flying back from Europe with a temperature around freezing and I had ended up with the flu because my lungs were not accustomed to breathing in such cold air while running at full tilt. Another time, during a Las Vegas layover, I had gone hiking in 100-degree heat with a hangover and no more than a bottle of water. I had stopped sweating and my heartbeat would not come down. I have had heat stroke twice from overdoing it. Yes, I have not always been the smartest when it comes to things like this, but I can say I have lived life to the fullest. I felt this fear was the cancer talking, trying to persuade me that I was no longer strong enough, that it was stronger than I. I thought back about all that I had survived and conquered, lots of chemo, radiation, two stem cell transplants, deep depression, and I started to laugh in cancer's face, I was laughing at fear itself. I thought of my favorite show, Naked and Afraid, a show in which two strangers, a man and a woman, are dumped in the middle of nowhere in very tough conditions like deserts, mountains and uninhabitable islands with only one tool each to get them through 21 days together. My daughter and I liked watching that show, and just the thought of walking through the desert without shoes (forget bra and panties, I would want some decent shoes) is enough for me to say no thank you. I wonder if these people could take on the stem cell transplant I had taken on, not once but twice in four months and I reminded myself that I, too, was a survivor and a strong one at that, both mentally and physically. As I was thinking these things I felt like the Myeloma was losing its grip on me. I imagined it lagging behind, I watched its energy leaving my body and dissipate into the air where it could do no harm. "The Universe has got you," I told myself. "You have already won this battle." There were a couple more turns, some wet and slippery patches before Coco and I made it to the top. When we got there I wanted to laugh, I wanted to cry. I felt overjoyed, at peace. I felt whole. The heck with the tests and numbers, I was healed already.

A little bit away from us stands a woman who passed us on the way up. She turns around and we say hi. I start telling her what I just accomplished, what I have lived through and why I am here. I want to cry with joy. I just want to share this moment with another human being. Her name is Joan, she is very kind and seems impressed. We shake hands and talk for a while. Her thoughts about holistic living is very much the same as mine. The only difference is that she believes chemo kills. "I used to think that too," I tell her," but that was before I had to either take it or die. Chemo saved my life!" I know this is something that is hard for a person to hear who feels holistically guided. Cancer and its journey has made me more moderate when it comes to medicine and alternative therapies. It has made me realize that we can and should take the best of all opportunities, let go of our judgments and step outside our box. She agrees. I tell her

I do everything healthy to keep my body and mind strong so that I can handle the chemo that still seems necessary to keep the cancer from taking over. Integration is good she agrees. I love it when my experience can open eyes.

We say our goodbyes and Coco and I make our journey back down. This time Coco walks, too. We take our time, I don't want us to slip and fall. On the way down many people are still making the climb up, most of them looking pretty tired. I cheer them on. "You are almost there," I say! I smile and make it a point to say hello to everybody. Today is a beautiful day! Today I conquered something very deep and profound. It always amazes me how much further I can still go. Even though I have come so far, there is always more for me to learn and higher for me to fly. Life is good indeed.

"I believe it is precisely because life doesn't last forever that we treasure it so much."

15

Coming Home

The two months in Colorado went by in a blink of an eye. Of course, while I was in the midst of it, alone in my little room with nothing else to do but lie on the bed and read, write and watch more Netflix movies than I care to admit, time seemed to stand still at times. I had wonderful moments, of course. I made deep friendships that will last a lifetime. I made an impact on others as they made on me. It continued to amaze me how well everything ended up fitting together. Granted, the beginning of the trip was a nightmare, but ultimately that just made for an interesting chapter. I was deeply disappointed that I could not take the gram of Rick Simpson Oil as was suggested. It was simply too difficult. Just two grains had me lying around with weird thoughts in my head, unable to do anything, including eating and taking care of myself. I decided that if this could truly cure people, it would have to be done in the same way a stem cell transplant is done, in a hospital under a doctor's supervision. That will be a long time coming, I am sure.

When I went back to MD Anderson my numbers had come down slightly, as had the tumor. Whether this was due to the cannabis or the new drug, I don't know. An x-ray did show that more of my rib was being destroyed and because of that my doctor decided to put me on a new drug that had just come out two months earlier. It was an immunotherapy drug which had a one in three chance of being successful. It would be a weekly infusion for eight weeks, followed by four months every other week, and then once a month until it would stop working, as all Multiple Myeloma drugs ultimately do because it is such a smart and adaptable cancer. I would continue to take the oral chemo, and I was excited and hopeful to get this started. Dr. R warned me that the first time could be rough but that patients usually responded well after that. After all I had gone through I was not concerned. I knew I would be in good hands and I did not count on any reactions. Boy, was I wrong.

Our first appointment was scheduled on a Monday. My husband went with me and we got ourselves settled in the room. We took some pictures of me being brave, with my arms up showing off my biceps. We had heard so much about this new generation of drugs that I fully believed this would be the one to put me in CR. The fact that it did not work in two thirds of the cases was something I chose not to think about. I was given Benadryl, steroids, and aspirin for premeds. The nurse had never done this therapy before, and she did not know what to expect. When they brought the bag in, it was huge. It must have been a gallon bag full of fluids. If everything went well it would take about six to eight hours. I started out at a low 50 mg. pace. Things looked good and I was nice and drowsy from the Benadryl. After an hour she increased the dose to 100 mg. Within about 10 minutes I started coughing. A little bit at first, but it became worse and worse. My husband called the nurse and when she came I had started wheezing and I felt my throat closing up. My nurse called in two more nurses and they gave me more Benadryl and steroids. My husband, in the meantime, started looking up symptoms for the treatment and saw that this was something that happened to patients the first time. He told our nurse who was apparently not brought up to speed on possible side effects. I was amazingly calm through the whole thing. I just wished she could have been, too. It took about 20 minutes for the coughing and wheezing to stop. After an hour she asked if I wanted to continue (she did not seem so sure herself). Absolutely, I wanted to continue. What was my choice here? Go home and watch my numbers go back up? At this point I had decided that if I was going to die, I would rather it be from chemo than the horrors and broken bones of Multiple Myeloma. Yes, the pain was that bad! I know this is not the case with some other cancers, and often when these patients choose to stop chemo their quality of life actually goes up. In the case of Multiple Myeloma this usually does not happen. Lying down while your bones break under your own weight is not the best way to go.

After an hour she increased me back to 100 mg, and this time I did great. When we went up to 150 mg. everything seemed okay, until I started to feel flustered and had to go to the bathroom. When I looked in the mirror I was all red and patchy and my face and neck were burning. I came back to the room and told my husband to get the nurse. Again we had to back off. I can't remember if I got more Benadryl because I was pretty drugged out at that time. She brought me back to 100 mg. and I stayed there for another hour. At this time, we had long passed the six-hour mark and we did not see an end in sight. The next time I was put back up to 150 mg. I did okay. The body is such an amazing organism. Its desire is to be in homeostasis is so strong that it will work very hard to keep us there, despite the abuse we put it through. I am very grateful for the way my body has carried me through these past three years! None of us was in a big hurry at this time, and we chose to keep it at 150 mg.

instead of pushing it to 200 mg. for the rest of the infusion. By the time we were done, 11 hours had passed. We had been taken to a different room because the part of the hospital we were in was closed for the night at 10:00 pm. We left the room at 1:00 am and were home by 2:00 am.

Our daughter had to have her first sleep over, something she did not want to do. She kept texting us throughout the evening to see how I was and when we would be home. She was tired but did not want to fall asleep. When we left and I texted her she did not respond. Thankfully, she had fallen asleep on the couch of our neighbor's house with her best friend. In the morning she was proud for having spent the night, and has since enjoyed a couple more sleepovers.

The next treatment went much smoother, though it was still a six-hour affair. As promised by my oncologist, the treatment happened without any further issues. After one month and four treatments the hour of truth was at hand. Did the immunotherapy work? I was really excited and nervous at the same time. So many times I had sat in Dr. R's office full of hope, then disappointed to find out that my numbers were not good. At other times, I had a bad month of feeling hopeless, only to find out that the numbers went down a lot. I had started to ponder this phenomenon. I'm a person who believes that thoughts are things that have an influence on our lives, and that we must be positive and affirm wholeness and health (something I certainly attempt do on a daily basis). Yet, it was curious to me that the numbers did not seem to agree with that way of thinking. I had started to wonder about a lot of things I had learned and I started to see my results as the "inconvenient truth" of the holistic society I had been part of for so long. Don't get me wrong, I still believe we should live in moderation, take good care of our bodies, and even more so our minds. But I also started to recognize a certain obsessiveness in the New Age and holistic thinking. God forbid you said "I will get better" because that is in the future, not the NOW. New Age people can be extremely scrutinizing and annoying. It is hard to live up to demands of perfection and having a normal conversation sometimes seems impossible.

I remember living downtown from the holistic place I worked at in Arizona. One of the girls working there was looking for a place downtown and she became my neighbor. She was very nice and quiet, with a serious disposition. I liked her. When she moved in, she was very particular how things had to be so she would stay peaceful and healthy. We had a neighbor behind us that smoked and liked rock and roll. I had never given his habits much thought but it drove her crazy. She thought it inconsiderate of him to be smoking outside and playing his music. The smoke did not bother me and the music wasn't bad. It's interesting that some seeking a spiritual or holistic lifestyle only seemed grounded while in their own little environment. I, on the other hand, lived a crazy life with kids on my days off (to make up for the Moms taking care of my daughter during the week while I worked). My house was messy, loud, and the door was always open for anybody to come in and say hello. Once again I realized that true peace can only come from within. If we need the outside and other people to behave in a certain way for us to be peaceful, we are not there yet. To be peaceful after a long hard day at work, coming home to hungry kids, and being happy making them a meal without worrying about the dishes afterwards, that is happiness and true inner peace, at least to me. I had not always been like that.... at all!! As a matter of fact, I was once very much like the other woman. I had compassion for her and knew she still had a bit of a way to go. I was very glad I wasn't like that anymore, though.

Dr. R came in and asked how I was feeling. "Great." I said, "But I want to see the results." He was very nonchalant about it, showing me one of my numbers; the Kappa Light chain, the immunoglobulins affected by the Myeloma, was in the normal range for the first time since diagnosed!!!! I was so excited. Other numbers weren't normal yet but I did not care. This therapy was working for me and that was all that mattered. One negative thing about this treatment was how it impacted my immune system. With numbers so low I had to get monthly shots to bring them back up again. Working at my little health food store was no longer a wise thing to do. Fortunately, I was working on my book, so I was keeping myself quite busy. I was given one week off after which time I would do another 4-weeks in a row. I was shocked when they checked my Kappa Light chains again at the beginning of the next session and they had almost tripled. It was disappointing to see how aggressive this Myeloma was, but after the next four treatments my numbers were once again in the normal range.

Last week I finished my fifth cycle and even though I now only have to go every other week, my numbers are still stable. I would be lying if I said I did not mind being on this treatment. I am so ready to get off it so my immune system can get a break and recover. At the same time, I do not want to see my numbers climb again, so I will do what I can to keep them down. My quality of life, other than needing to be cautious in public, is good. I hurt, but that is nothing new to me. I try to take as few drugs as I can. However, I no longer fear them and I will not suffer needlessly. I will continue to fight for the right to use cannabis so that we can choose how we wish to treat our nausea, our depression, anxiety, and pain. Of course, my story is long from over and you have not heard the last of me. But here we are today.

May 21, 2016
Cherie Rineker

"Writing has been the best kind of therapy money never could have bought me."

Epilogue

Where Do I Go from Here?

Does this book have a happy ending? That depends on what your definition of "happy" is. If you mean by happy that even with all my positivity, prayers and meditation I am now cured, the answer is no. To this day I am still doing treatments. As a matter of fact, as I am writing down these words, it is almost 8.30 PM and I am sitting in bed at MD Anderson for an appointment that was supposed to start at 9:00 am this morning but didn't start until about 4:00 pm. I am okay with that, because it allowed me to write a book chapter, talk to some great friends, and take a nice nap. I still feel the physical effects of the destruction both the cancer and the chemo has done to me. I no longer look at happiness through the eyes of an innocent child who believes that the world is only good if everything goes her way. I have gone through too much to think this, and that is okay with me. I have fallen too deep and hurt too much. I am grateful for the lessons my life has taught me because they have made me wiser, more tolerant, and sympathetic to the pains of all kinds of people and problems. I have been able to shed my empathetic feelings as I see no need in taking on other people's hurt any longer. They are not served by my holding their pain neither am I. While I sympathize with people who feel they are suffering, this is different than taking on the problems and pain of the world like I used to. It is not required of us and nothing can be gained from that.

Though I would not wish my journey on my worst enemy, I know there are people in this world that would benefit from the trials I have gone through. But only if they too are willing to humble themselves and gain the wisdom that has come from experiencing these vulnerable places. It is so important that we don't look at ourselves as victims. While at the same time realizing that we cannot have control over every situation, not even our own feeling sometimes. This is when we must surrender and accept that which is at hand with the belief that tomorrow can bring us a better day. There is strength in every one of us, if we choose to look deep enough. We have a strength and adaptability which allows us to deal with the toughest of circumstances and come out stronger than we ever thought possible. To do this we must give up our desire to blame. Personal responsibility is an absolute must. I was not responsible for the actions of my parents. The fact that I started out life with so much stacked against me was unfair indeed, but it was as it was. What I ended up doing with my life was my responsibility. I tried a decade of blaming and victimhood, another one of anger and whining. Ultimately I got tired of the person I had become and I wanted more for myself. Being a victim, though it got me sympathy, no longer worked for me. Besides, who wants to hang around someone who is stuck in the past, unable to appreciate today? The steps I had to go through were steps of grieving and growth. I do not blame myself for taking this long, but I sure am glad I got over it. For me it took removing my parents and sisters from my life. Maybe you can salvage your relationships. You may ask if I regret making that choice. Although I do wish I could have a "normal" relationship with my family, this was simply not possible. I am at peace with where I am these days.

I hope this book has managed to do for you what it did for me. To let you see that no matter the circumstances in your life, there is always hope as long as we continue to believe there is. Hang on for another day. Go out and knock on your neighbor's door. Bring over some cookies and start smiling at people. Believe me, most people will smile back! So many of us feel alone and are simply afraid to go out and connect. Open up your heart, no matter how many times it has been broken, because the other option is to go at life alone and that is no option at all.

I will leave you with a letter I wrote to cancer during my Colorado stay. Though the Myeloma is still hanging around, I do see a future where this will no longer will be the case. But if not, then that is okay, too.

Good bye Cancer,

I am writing you this letter today because I want to thank you. I want to thank you for the many lessons you have taught me. Thank you for allowing me to see that I have the best life ever!

You taught me that no matter what comes my way, I can handle it. It is because of you that I realized that by helping others I am helping myself.

It is because of you that I know my life truly matters. Though you had a grip on my body, you couldn't steal my soul.

You allowed me to let go of the people that weren't healthy in my life. This gave me lots of space for people that could see the best in me. You did not cripple my Love, you allowed me to feel it even more fully. Though you tried to shatter my Hope, you failed in that I have more faith now than I ever had.

By allowing me to look death straight in the eyes, you took away my fear of death and replaced it with a deep Inner Peace.

My friendships are stronger than ever and there is not a soul in this world that I do not consider my friend and teacher.

You gave me a cause to fight for, a fight for freedom of choice, for all sick people in all states, to have the right to fight for their lives in any way they see fit, without a government to take that right away.

So cancer, thank you for all your lessons. I have paid attention to them and I have learned from them. I have walked away with way more than I started with, and it is with gratitude that I bid you farewell. You are no longer needed in this body of mine. You are no longer needed in my life.

Cherie

Resources

www.cherierineker.com   lievie007@yahoo.com

G Whitcoe Designs - *www.gwhitcoedesigns.com* – *Graphic Design, Web Design and Fine Art.*

Hands 4 Hope Project, Inc. is a 501 (c) (3) organization that accepts donations to help those living with a cancer diagnosis receive massage therapy. *Www.hands4hopeproject.org,*

508 S. Independence Blvd. Suite 101, Virginia Beach, VA 23452, P: 757-434-9664

Hands4hopeproject@gmail.com

National Hemp Association (NHA) is a 501 c (4) non-profit trade association dedicated to the rebirth of the industrial hemp industry in the U.S. – 1460 Quince Ave., #102, Boulder, CO 80304; (303) 413-8066. www. NationalHempAssociation.org.

NHA has three missions: to **educate** about the many uses of hemp; **advocate** for legislation at the state and federal level to make hemp fully legal; and **connect** people, hemp businesses and organizations so hemp can again be a major American crop that U.S. farmers can grow for U.S. hemp products. NHA offers a variety of membership levels (individual, farmer, business, investor and state affiliate) and is building a growing network of citizen leaders and advocates across the nation.

David B. Bush, L.L.C. d/b/a **David Law**. David Bush is an experienced business and commercial litigation attorney providing legal advice and assistance to the emerging industrial hemp economy in Colorado and other states.
1:303-422-0064 (office)
www.davidlawcolorado.com
bush@davidlawcolorado.com

Cherie lives with her husband and daughter in South East Texas. She is currently working on her next book, and continues treatment at MD Anderson with Hope for the future.

Her education is in Holistic Health. Graduate of Cayce Reilly school of Massotherapy and SWINA (South West Institute of Natural Esthetics).

Made in the USA
San Bernardino, CA
01 March 2017